English Traditional Songs
and Carols

ENGLISH TRADITIONAL SONGS AND CAROLS,

COLLECTED AND EDITED,

WITH

ANNOTATIONS AND PIANOFORTE ACCOMPANIMENTS,

BY

LUCY E. BROADWOOD.

EP PUBLISHING LIMITED
ROWMAN & LITTLEFIELD
TOTOWA, NEW JERSEY
1974

Copyright © in reprint 1974 EP Publishing Limited
First published Boosey & Co, London, 1908

This edition published 1974 by EP Publishing Limited
East Ardsley, Wakefield
Yorkshire, England

First published in the United States 1974 by
Rowman and Littlefield
Totowa, New Jersey

ISBN 0 7158 1025 1 (EP Publishing)

ISBN 0-87471-542-3 (Rowman & Littlefield)

Please address all enquiries to EP Publishing Limited
(address as above)

Printed and bound in Great Britain by
REDWOOD BURN LIMITED
Trowbridge & Esher

INDEX.

TITLE	COUNTY	PAGE
Abdication (Boney's)	Sussex	34
Ages of Man (The)	Do.	20
Banstead Downs	Do.	32
Bedfordshire May-Day Carol	Bedfordshire	84
Belfast Mountains	Sussex	36
Bold Pedlar and Robin Hood (The)	Do.	4
Boney's Lamentation	Do.	34
Brisk young Lad, he courted me (A)	North Lincolnshire	92
Brisk young lively Lad (The)	Surrey	72
Bristol Town	Sussex	10
Cold blows the Wind	North Devonshire	54
Constant Farmer's Son (The)	Sussex	28
Death and the Lady	Do.	40
Died of Love	North Lincolnshire	92
Duke of Marlborough (The)	Sussex	22
Gallant Poachers (The)	Do.	2
Georgie	Do.	32
Gibson, Wilson, and Johnson	Do.	42
Hampshire Mummers' Christmas Carol	Hampshire	78
Henry Martin	Sussex	30
How cold the Winds do blow	Surrey	50, 52
I must live all alone	Sussex	16
Irish Girl (The)	Surrey	60
King Henry, my Son	Cumberland	96
King Pharaoh (Gypsy Christmas Carol)	Sussex and Surrey	74
Little Lowland Maid (The)	Surrey	66
Lost Lady found (The)	Lincolnshire	86
Merchant's Daughter (The)	Sussex	28
Moon shines bright (The) (Christmas Carol)	Sussex and Surrey	76
New Irish Girl (The)	Surrey	60
Oh, the Trees are getting high	Do.	56
Oh, Yarmouth is a pretty Town	Sussex	102
Our Ship she lies in Harbour	Surrey	58
Poor murdered Woman (The)	Do.	70
Rich Nobleman and his Daughter (The)	Do.	68
Rosetta and her gay Ploughboy	Sussex	18
Salt Seas	Do.	30
Some Rival has stolen my true Love away	Surrey	108
Sussex Mummers' Christmas Carol (The)	Sussex	80
Three Butchers (The)	Do.	42
Through Moorfields	Do.	6
Travel the Country round	Do.	100
Two affectionate Lovers (The)	Do.	38
Unquiet Grave (The)	Surrey	50, 52
Do.	North Devonshire	54
Valiant Lady (The)	Surrey	72
Van Diemen's Land	Sussex	2
Wealthy Farmer's Son (The)	Do.	26
Young Servant Man (The)	Do.	38

INDEX TO FIRST LINES.

	PAGE
A brisk young lad came courting me	92
Abroad as I was walking	60
All on the Belfast Mountains	36
As I rode over Banstead Downs	32
As I was a-walking one morning by chance	16
A story I will tell to you	42
Attend, you sons of high renown	34
Cold blows the wind	54
Come all you gallant poachers	2
Come all you pretty fair maids	26
Fair lady, throw those costly robes aside	40
How cold the winds do blow	50, 52
I am a jovial ranger	100
In Bristol Town, as I have heard tell	10
In prime of years, when I was young	20
It's of a brisk young lively lad	72
It's of a damsel both fair and handsome	38
It's of a merchant's daughter	28
It's of a pretty sailor lad	66
It's of a rich nobleman	68
It was Hankey, the Squire	70
I've been rambling all the night	84
King Pharaoh sat a-musing	74
Oh, the moon shines bright	76
Oh, the trees are getting high	56
Oh, where have you been wandering	96
Oh, Yarmouth is a pretty town	102
Our ship she lies in harbour	58
Some rival has stolen my true love away	108
There chanced to be a pedlar bold	4
There is six good days all in the week	78
There were three brothers in merry Scotland	30
Through Moorfields and to Bedlam I went	6
'Twas down in a valley a fair maid did dwell	86
When righteous Joseph wedded was	80
You constant lovers, give attention	18
You generals all, and champions bold	22

"Music is the true universal speech of mankind."

—C. von Weber.

"Music is the poor man's Parnassus."

—Emerson.

"Poetry, were it the rudest, so it be sincere, is the attempt which man makes to render his existence harmonious, the utmost he can do for that end; it springs therefore from his whole feelings, opinions, activity, and takes its character from these. It may be called the music of the whole inner being."

—Carlyle.

"National music, be it ever so artless and simple, is in most cases what music in the first place always ought to be—a faithful expression of feelings . . . . The shepherd tending his flock, the soldier on the march, the fisherman mending his nets, the labourer in the cornfield, has no inducement to sing his favourite tune unless his heart's emotions incite him to it. His musical effusions emanate therefore from the heart, or, in other words, they are psychologically true."

—C. Engel.

PREFACE.

THE words on the preceding page seem to account all-sufficiently for the existence of popular traditional music and verse, their strength and their weakness.

The strength of traditional melodies is indeed almost undeniable. Originally the perfectly sincere expression of some musical soul, they have passed on from father to son, receiving the impress of simple music-lovers unaccustomed to harmony, and therefore the more critically alive to the essentials of fine melody.

It should not surprise us that the weakness of folk-song is most often apparent in its verse. A child will sing before it can speak. To compose a noble melody without harmony needs no teacher; whereas the invention of good poetry presupposes a varied vocabulary, a knowledge of grammar and the rules of rhyme and rhythm, and, above all, that habit of eloquence in daily speech and thought bred solely of familiarity with books. And books, even in their simplest form, were often unknown to the country dwellers through whom these old songs have descended.

Bearing this in mind we shall deal more justly with the doggerel narrative, faulty rhyme, and irregular metre of the country ballad. The most grotesque, when analyzed, will often prove to contain dramatic or noble elements in awkward disguise. Take, for example, "The Merchant's Daughter" in this collection: its plot is the same as that of the old story made famous by Boccaccio, versified by Hans Sachs, and immortalised by Keats in his poem "Isabella, or the Pot of Basil."

But, if traditional country verse has its weakness it also has its strength. Such a line as "Oh, love it is a killing thing! did you ever feel the pain?" lives in the memory of the hearer long after the old singer has passed away. There is something hauntingly beautiful in a verse such as this one from the "Bedfordshire May-Day Carol":—

> "When I am dead, and in my grave,
> And covered with cold clay,
> The nightingale will sit and sing,
> And pass the time away."

Burns, an inspired peasant himself, perceived these beauties in peasant poetry, and some of his sincerest and most famous lines are taken from homely ballads, familiar to the unlettered country singer and to most collectors of traditional song.

The words of many country ballads are derived, directly or indirectly, from broadsides. The invention of printing early gave birth to these, which recorded both the orally-traditional and newly-made ballads of the strolling minstrel and tavern-bard. Before the days of cheap literature, the broadside, indeed, took the place of the newspaper, political pamphlet, history, novel, poetry-book, and hymnal of our times; and upon the ballad-sheets—largely circulated by pedlars, themselves often singers—the country folk relied for fresh information, amusement, and moral instruction, the more easily assimilated when in homely verse.

With cheaper printing, there poured forth from the provincial presses an ever-swelling tide of broadsides, still bearing ballads taken from the lips of singers and local rhymesters ignorant of literary conventions.

Many ballads were common to most broadside printers, but the versions of these, as given by different publishers, are rarely identical. Indeed, the kaleidoscopic shifting of lines or whole verses, the additions, curtailments, borrowings, diversity of metre, and the strange corruptions in these printed versions (ancient or modern), go to prove that, however much the country singer or local bard may be beholden—directly or indirectly—to the broadside,* the broadside is equally indebted to the ballad-singer and hedge-poet.

"Seven Dials" is often rightly credited with having turned out feeble stuff of the "Villikins and his Dinah" type; but, on the other hand, the astute Northumbrian printer, James Catnach, (settled in London 1813), paid men to collect ballads from singers in country taverns; and there exists a serious broadside, "William and Diana," which is older than his burlesqued version, if hardly of greater literary merit. There is no doubt that other printers followed Catnach's plan, and this offers the only satisfactory explanation of the fluidity of traditional ballads throughout long centuries.

It must not be forgotten that the process of composing tunes and words is still going on amongst unsophisticated people, and in the British Isles. It is most noticeable amongst the more eloquent Celtic peasants of Scotland, Ireland and Wales, but the non-Celtic Scots of Yarrowside have preserved their poetical traditions, and still naturally express their emotions in verse. The more reticent and slow-tongued Englishman of limited education is often ill-pleased enough to be discovered a bard, but he not unfrequently makes tunes, or verse, of a kind.† I have myself met with several instances; and, as a child, was often privileged to read the valentines and letters in rhyme composed by a friendly Sussex bard, at the request of less poetical but love-sick swains.

Given the ballad, the metre and character of its words suggested an appropriate tune to the singer, who, recalling ballad-airs learnt usually from persons of an older generation, altered and adorned them according to his fancy, producing in traditional music similar kaleidoscopic changes to those through which the ballad itself had passed.

Thirty-four of the songs in this book represent a very small selection from a number noted and collected by myself, chiefly in Sussex and Surrey and between the years 1893 and 1901. To these are added five noted by others. In selecting for publication I preferred such songs as had already undergone my more leisurely examination and annotation. All editorial notes appear here in greatly condensed form, and references are necessarily very incomplete.

Every tune in the book is faithful to the version noted from the singer at the time named.

The original words of the singers remain also unaltered, save in trifling instances where a false rhyme, forgotten line, nonsensical corruption, or the like, has made it absolutely necessary to correct them. Each singer of these versions has thus the opportunity of being his own editor, and may compress or modify according to his individual taste, as the country singer has done before him. In two cases a verse has been omitted, and the wording of a line slightly changed. One song has been partly re-written, as stated elsewhere. The unaltered words may in many cases be found in the *Journal of the Folk Song Society*, together with various details omitted here.

---

* The broadside flourished from the early sixteenth century to the middle of the nineteenth, and still languishes in a debased form.
† See "The Poor Murdered Woman," p. 70.

The singers to whom I am indebted for songs in this collection are:—

1. Mr. GRANTHAM, an old carter, of the Holmwood, Surrey, now dead. He was a native of Sussex, and learned his songs from other carters and labourers. He could not read.

2. Mr. FOSTER, a young farm labourer of Milford, Surrey.

3. Messrs. BAKER, BROMHAM, EDE, LOUGH AND SPARKS, all farm-labourers, mostly over fifty years of age, in the village and neighbourhood of Dunsfold, Surrey.

4. Mrs. RUGMAN, wife of a labourer in Dunsfold, Surrey.

5. A GYPSY FAMILY OF THE NAME OF GOBY, wanderers in Sussex and Surrey.

6. Mr. WALTER SEARLE, a young quarryman, near Amberley, Sussex.

7. Mr. HENRY BURSTOW, a shoemaker, born in Horsham, 1826. As a boy he was apprenticed to the shoemaking trade, but is best known as a bell-ringer. It has lately been written of him that his reputation "stands unrivalled in England, and there is hardly a belfry in the land where his name and fame are not known and respected." And this, although during eighty-three years he has slept only six nights away from his native town. Mr. Burstow has from childhood made bell-ringing and song-singing his hobbies. He has a list of more than four hundred songs, old and new, which he knows by heart. Amongst them about fifty or sixty are of the traditional ballad type, and these have been noted and preserved. Mr. Burstow learned some of his songs from his parents, and many "old songs and ballets off shoemakers singing at their work." Others he learned from labourers, many of whom could not read. His excellent ear and sense of rhythm have probably been developed by constant bell-ringing, in which he still joins (in 1908), with energy and skill.

8. Mr. JOSEPH TAYLOR, estate bailiff, of Saxby-All-Saints, North Lincolnshire; born in Binbrook, Lincs., 1833. He has been a choirman in his village for forty-two years, but familiarity with modern major and minor scales has not destroyed his power of singing purely modal tunes. His voice is a flexible true tenor, and his genius for delicately ornamenting his melodies, whilst exquisitely preserving the rhythm, is one which many a skilled musican might envy.

9. Mrs. HILLS, an old family nurse; native of Stamford, Lincolnshire.

10. Mrs. JEFFREYS, an old cottager in North Devonshire, now deceased.

11. Mrs. THORBURN (Margaret Scott), native of Cumberland; formerly in service.

I must again express gratitude to the singers whose kindness and patience have made the task of collecting so pleasant. My thanks are also offered to the following, for valuable help of various kinds:—Mr. W. Albery, Mr. G. Arkwright, Miss C. Burne, Mr. Buttifant, Mrs. H. Carr, Sir Ernest Clarke, Mr. H. E. D. Hammond, Mr. F. Kidson, Miss M. B. Lattimer, Mr. C. A. Lidgey, the Rev. E. J. Nash, and the Rev. C. J. Shebbeare.

Beginners in the study of Folk Song, who may wish for more information than that scattered throughout the prefaces of published collections, will find the following useful: "Purity in Music," A. F. Thibaut; "The Study of National Music," Carl Engel; "The Literature of National Music," Carl Engel; "The Art of Music" (opening chapters), C. Hubert Parry; "The History of Music in England" (concluding chapter), Ernest Walker; "Popular Music of the Olden Time," W. Chappell; "English Folk Song," Cecil Sharp; "Rhythm in National Music," T. H. Yorke Trotter, and "On the Collecting of English Folk Song," L. E. Broadwood, (*Proceedings of the Musical Association, 1904–1905*); "The Ballad Sheet and Garland," F. Kidson (*Journal of the Folk Song Society*, Vol. ii., No. 7); "Folk Song in Buchan," Gavin Greig, (an essay printed by P. Scrogie, "Buchan Observer Office," Peterhead, N.B.); "Grove's Dictionary of Music," (*see* "Modes," "Song," etc.).

LUCY E. BROADWOOD,
84, CARLISLE MANSIONS,
LONDON, S.W.

July, 1908.

English Traditional Songs
and
Carols.

Van Diemen's Land.
or The Gallant Poachers.

[DORIAN.] [SUSSEX.]

Allegro e ben marcato.

Come, all you gallant poachers, that ramble free from care, That walk out of a moonlight night, with your dog, your gun and snare; Where the {lofty / lusty} hare and pheasant you have at your command, Not thinking that your last career is on Van Diemen's Land!

Verses 1-7.

Copyright 1908 by Boosey & Co. H.5873.

1.
Come, all you gallant poachers, that ramble free from care,
That walk out of a moonlight night, with your dog, your gun, and snare;
Where the {lofty / lusty} hare and pheasant you have at your command,
Not thinking that your last career is on Van Diemen's Land.

2.
There was poor Tom Brown from Nottingham, Jack Williams, and poor Joe,
Were three as daring poachers as the country well does know;
At night they were trapannèd by the keepers hid in sand,
And for fourteen years transported were unto Van Diemen's Land.

3.
Oh! when we sailed from England we landed at the bay,
We had rotten straw for bedding, we dared not to say nay.
Our cots were fenced with fire, (we slumber when we can,)
To drive away the wolves and tigers upon Van Diemen's Land.

4.
Oh! when that we were landed upon that fatal shore,
The planters they came flocking round, full twenty score or more;
They ranked us up like horses, and sold us out of hand,
They yoked us to the plough, my boys, to plough Van Diemen's Land.

5.
There was one girl from England, Susan Summers was her name,
For fourteen years transported was, we all well knew the same;
Our planter bought her freedom, and he married her out of hand,
Good usage then she gave to us, upon Van Diemen's Land.

6.
Oh! oft when I am slumbering, I have a pleasant dream:
With my sweet girl I am sitting, down by some purling stream,
Through England I am roaming, with her at my command,
Then waken, brokenhearted, upon Van Diemen's Land.

7.
God bless our wives and families, likewise that happy shore,
That isle of sweet contentment which we shall see no more.
As for our wretched females, see them we seldom can,
There are twenty to one woman upon Van Diemen's Land.

8.
Come all you gallant poachers, give ear unto my song,
It is a bit of good advice, although it is not long:
Lay by your dog and snare; to you I do speak plain,
If you knew the hardships we endure you ne'er would poach again.

[Sung by Mr H. Burstow, 1893.]

See Appendix page 113

The Bold Pedlar and Robin Hood.

[DORIAN Influence.] [SUSSEX.]

1

There chanced to be a Pedlar bold,
    A Pedlar bold there chanced to be;
He put his pack all on his back,
    And so merrily trudgèd o'er the lea.

2

By chance he met two troublesome men,
    Two troublesome men they chanced to be,
The one of them was bold Robin Hood,
    And the other was little John so free.

3

"O Pedlar, Pedlar, what is in thy pack?
    Come speedily and tell to me."
"I've several suits of the gay green silks,
    And silken bowstrings by two or three."

4

"If you have several suits of the gay green silk,
    And silken bowstrings two or three,
Then, by my body," cries little John,
    "One half your pack shall belong to me."

5

"O nay, O nay," said the Pedlar bold,
    "O nay, O nay, that never can be,
For there's never a man from fair Nottingham,
    Can take one half my pack from me."

6

Then the Pedlar he pulled off his pack,
    And put it a little below his knee,
Saying, "If you do move me one perch from this,
    My pack and all shall gang with thee."

7

Then little John he drew his sword,
    The Pedlar by his pack did stand,
They fought until they both did sweat,
    Till he cried, "Pedlar, pray hold your hand."

8

Then Robin Hood he was standing by,
    And he did laugh most heartily,
Saying, "I could find a man of smaller scale,
    Could thrash the Pedlar and also thee."

9

"Go you try, master," says little John,
    "Go you try, master, most speedily,
For by my body," says little John,
    "I am sure this night you will know me."

10

Then Robin Hood he drew his sword,
    And the Pedlar by his pack did stand;
They fought till the blood in streams did flow,
    Till he cried, "Pedlar, pray hold your hand.

11

O Pedlar, Pedlar, what is thy name?
    Come speedily and tell to me."
"Come, my name I ne'er will tell,
    Till both your names you have told to me."

12

"The one of us is bold Robin Hood,
    And the other little John so free."
"Now," says the Pedlar, "it lays to my good will,
    Whether my name I choose to tell to thee.

13

I am Gamble Gold of the gay green woods,
    And travelled far beyond the sea,
For killing a man in my father's land,
    And from my country was forced to flee."

14

"If you are Gamble Gold of the gay green woods,
    And travelled far beyond the sea,
You are my mother's own sister's son,
    What nearer cousins can we be?"

15

They sheathed their swords, with friendly words,
    So merrily they did agree,
They went to a tavern and there they dined,
    And cracked bottles most merrily.

[*Sung by Mr H. Burstow, 1893.*]

Through Moorfields.

1.

Through Moorfields, and to Bedlam I went;
I heard a young damsel to sigh and lament;
She was wringing of her hands, and tearing of her hair,
Crying "Oh! cruel parents! you have been too severe!

2.

You've banished my truelove o'er the seas away,
Which causes me in Bedlam to sigh, and to say
That your cruel, base actions cause me to complain,
For the loss of my dear has distracted my brain."

3.

When the silk-mercer first came on shore,
As he was passing by Bedlam's door,
He heard his truelove lamenting full sore,
Saying "Oh! I shall never see him any more!"

4.

The mercer, hearing that, he was struck with surprise,
When he saw through the window her beautiful eyes;
He ran to the porter the truth for to tell,
Saying "Show me the way to the joy of my soul!"

5.

The porter on the mercer began for to stare,
To see how he was for the loss of his dear;
He gave to the porter a broad piece of gold,
Saying "Show me the way to the joy of my soul!"

6.

And when that his darling jewel he did see
He took her, and sat her all on his knee,
Says she "Are you the young man my father sent to sea,
My own dearest jewel, for loving of me?"

7.

"Oh yes! I'm the man that your father sent to sea,
Your own dearest jewel, for loving of thee!"
"Then adieu to my sorrows, for they now are all fled,
Adieu to these chains, and likewise this straw bed!"

8.

They sent for their parents, who came then with speed;
They went to the church, and were married indeed.
So all you wealthy parents, do a warning take,
And never strive true lovers their promises to break.

[*Sung by Mr H. Burstow, 1893.*]

See Appendix page 113.

Bristol Town.

1.

In Bristol Town, as I have heard tell,
A rich merchant there did dwell.
He had a daughter beautiful and bright,
On her he fixed his own heart's delight.

2.

Courted she was by many in the town,
Courted she was by many a clever man,
Courted she was by many a clever man,
But none could this young lady's heart gain.

3.

Till a brisk young sailor he came from the seas,
He did the lady well please.
He was a brisk young man although a sailor poor,
And the lady did the sailor adore.

4.

And when her father came for to be told
She was courted by this jolly sailor bold,
"No! never, never, oh! while I do live,
Not any portion unto you I'll give!"

5.

"As for your portion I do not care,
I'll wed the man whom I love so dear,
I'll wed the man that I do love so,
If along with him a-begging I go!"

6.

Her father kept a valiant servant man,
Who wrote a letter out of hand;
This letter was the sailor to invite
To meet her in the valley by night.

7.

Her father kept a valiant Irishman,
And fifty pounds he gave him out of hand,
And a brace of pocket pistols likewise,
He mounted, and away he did ride.

8.

He mounted and away he did ride,
Till at length the jolly sailor he espied,
At length the jolly sailor he spied there,
A-waiting for his joy and his dear.

9.

He said "I am come to kill you indeed,
Away! back to some tavern with speed;
Cheer up your heart with bowls of good wine,
And soon I'll make you know my design:

10.

I will go back to my master with speed,
Saying "Master, I have killed that man, indeed!
I have buried him all in his grave so low,
Where streams and fountains over him do flow."

11.

In course of time the rich merchant died,
Which filled the lady's heart full with pride;
Now she's married to that man, you know, so brave,
Who her father thought was dead, and in his grave.

[*Sung by M.r H. Burstow, 1893.*]

I must live all alone.

[SUSSEX]

1
As I was a-walking one morning by chance,
　I heard a maid making her moan,
I asked why she sighed, and she sadly replied
　　"Alas! I must live all alone, alone,
　　Alas! I must live all alone."

2
I said "My fair maid, pray whence have you strayed?
　And are you some distance from home?"
"My home," replied she "is a burden to me,
　　For there I must live all alone, alone,
　　For there I must live all alone.

3
When I was eleven, sweethearts I had seven,
　And then I would look upon none;
But now all in vain I must sigh and complain,
　　For my true love has left me alone, alone,
　　For my true love has left me alone,

4
Oh! come back from sea, my dear Johnny, to me,
　And make me a bride of your own!
Or else for your sake my poor heart it will break,
　　And here I shall die all alone, alone,
　　And here I shall die all alone."

[Sung by Mr H. Burstow, 1893.]

Rosetta and her gay Ploughboy.

1

You constant lovers give attention
   While a tale to you I tell,
Concerning of two lovers true,
   Who in one house for years did dwell:
Rosetta was a farmer's daughter,
   And always was her parents' joy,
Till Cupid in a snare had caught her,
   With her father's gay ploughboy.

2

At break of day each summer's morning
   William for his horses went,
And as he viewed bright Phoebus dawning,
   He would listen with content
To the voice of sweet Rosetta,
   Which charmed young William's heart with joy;
With voice so shrill she loved young Will,
   Who was her father's gay plough boy.

3

She sat and sung of her sweet William,
   As she milked her spotted cow;
And he would sigh for his Rosetta
   All the day while at the plough;
And as evening did approach,
   Rosetta tript along with joy,
With voice so shrill, to meet young Will,
   Who was her father's gay ploughboy.

4

Her father came into the dairy,
   While she sung her tale of love,
He fixed his eyes to her surprise,
   And swore by all the powers above
That he was told the hussy bold
   Along with poverty did toy,
And that long time she had been courting
   Of young Will, her gay ploughboy.

5

Rosetta said "My dearest father,
   Shall I speak with courage bold?
I milk my cow, I love the plough,
   I value William more than gold."
Then in a cellar he confined her,
   Where no one could her annoy,
And with delight, both day and night,
   She sighed for Will, her gay ploughboy.

6

Fifteen long months on bread and water
   Sweet Rosetta was confined,
So fast in love had Cupid caught her,
   No one thing could change her mind.
Her father strove with all his might
   Her happiness for to destroy,
But nothing could Rosetta daunt,
   She doated on her gay ploughboy.

7

At length grim death her father summoned
   From this sinful world of care,
And then to his estate and fortune
   Rosetta was the only heir.
Then she and William were united,
   No one could their peace destroy,
The village bells did call Rosetta,
   And young Will, her gay ploughboy.

8

For miles around the lads and lasses
   Merrily for them did sing,
At their wedding all was joyful,
   And the village bells did ring.
No couple can be more contented,
   Their happiness none can destroy,
They sing with joy "God speed the plough,"
   Rosetta and her gay ploughboy.

[*Sung by Mr H. Burstow, 1893.*]

The Ages of Man.

[MIXOLYDIAN.] [SUSSEX.]

In prime of years, when I was young, I took delight in youthful toys, Not knowing then what did belong Unto the pleasure of those days. At sev'n years old I was a child, And subject for to be beguiled.

1

In prime of years, when I was young,
I took delight in youthful toys,
Not knowing then what did belong
Unto the pleasure of those days.
At seven years old I was a child,
And subject for to be beguiled.

2

At twice seven, I must needs go learn
What discipline was taught at school;
When good from evil I could discern
I thought myself no more a fool.
My parents were contriving then
How I might live when {I became / grown} a man.

3

At three times seven, I wexèd wild,
And manhood led me to be bold;
I thought myself no more a child,
My own conceit it so me told.
Then I did venture far and near
To buy delight at price full dear.

4

At four times seven {I must take a wife / I must wive}
And leave off all my wanton ways,
Thinking thereby perhaps to thrive
And save myself from sad disgrace.
So fare ye well, companions all,
For other business doth me call.

5

At five times seven, I would go prove
What I could gain by art or skill;
But still against the stream I strove,
I bowled stones up against the hill.
The more I laboured with might and main,
The more I strove, {against the stream. / and strove in vain.}

6

At six times seven, all covetness
Began to harbour in my breast,
My mind then still contriving was
How I might gain all worldly wealth,
To purchase lands, and live on them,
To make my children mighty men.

7

At seven times seven, all worldly care
Began to harbour in my brain;
Then I did drink a heavy draught
Of water of experience plain.
Then none so ready was as I,
To purchase, bargain, sell, or buy.

8

At eight times seven, I wexèd old,
I took myself unto my rest;
My neighbours then my counsel craved
And I was held in great request.
But age did so abate my strength
That I was forced to yield at length.

9

At nine times seven, I must take leave
Of all my carnal {vain delight, / vanity,}
And then full sore it did me grieve,
I fetched up many a bitter sigh.
To rise up early, and sit up late
{I was no longer fit, my strength did abate. / I was not fit, strength did abate.}

10

At ten times seven, my glass was run,
And I, poor silly man, must die,
I lookèd up, and saw the sun
Was overcome with crystal sky.
And now I must this world forsake,
Another man my place must take.

11

Now you may see within the glass
The whole estate of mortal man;
How they from seven to seven do pass,
Until they are three score and ten,
And, when their glass is fully run,
They (must) leave off where they first begun.

[*Sung by M? H. Burstow, 1893.*]

The Duke of Marlborough.

always fought with merry men, But now to Death must yield! 2. I
many towns I often took, I did the world surprise. 3. King

8ves. ad libitum

Charles the Second I did serve, To face our foes in France, And
we have gained the victory, And bravely kept the field, We've

at the battle of Ramilies We boldly did advance;
took a number of prisoners And forced them to yield.

The sun was down, the earth did shine, So loudly I did cry: Fight
That very day My horse was shot, All by a musket ball; As

8ves. ad libitum

on, my brave boys, For England! We'll conquer, or we'll nobly die! 4. Now
I was mounting up again My aide-de-camp did fall. 5. Now

8ves ad lib.

H.5873.

24

Last verse

on..... a bed..... of sickness laid I am resigned to die. Yet generals all, and champions bold, Stand true as well as I: Take no bribes! Stand true to your colours! And fight with courage bold! I have led my men...... through fire and smoke, But ne'er was bribed with gold.

H.5873.

1.

You generals all, and champions bold,
    That take delight in the field,
That knock down palaces and castle walls,
    But now to Death must yield.
Oh! I must go and face the foe,
    With sword and shield;
I always fought with merry men,
    But now to Death must yield.

2.

I am an Englishman by my birth,
    And Marlborough is my name,
In Devonshire I drew my breath,
    That place of noted fame;
I was beloved by all my men,
    Kings and Princes likewise;
Though many towns I often took,
    I did the world surprise.

3.

King Charles the Second I did serve,
    To face our foes in France,
And at the battle of Ramilies
    We boldly did advance;
The sun was down, the earth did shine,
    So loudly I did cry:
"Fight on, my brave boys, for England,—
    We'll conquer, or we'll nobly die!"

4.

Now we have gained the victory,
    And bravely kept the field,
We've took a number of prisoners,
    And forcèd them to yield.
That very day my horse was shot,
    All by a musket ball;
As I was mounting up again
    My aide-de-camp did fall.

5.

Now on a bed of sickness laid,
    I am resigned to die;
Yet generals all, and champions bold,
    Stand true as well as I:
Take no bribes! stand true to your colours!
    And fight with courage bold!
I have led my men through fire and smoke,
    But ne'er was bribed with gold.

[Sung by Mr H. Burstow, 1893]

The Wealthy Farmer's Son.

[SUSSEX.]

Allegro.

Come all you pretty fair maids, and listen to my song, While I relate a story that does to love belong. 'Tis of a blooming damsel walked through the fields so gay, And there she met her true love, And he unto her did say:

H.5873.

1.
Come all you pretty fair maids, and listen to my song,
While I relate a story that does to love belong:
'Tis of a blooming damsel walked through the fields so gay,
And there she met her true love, and he unto her did say:

2.
"Where are you going, young Nancy, this morning bright and gay?
Or why do you walk here alone? Come tell to me, I pray."
"I am going to yonder river-side, where fishes they do swim,
All for to gather flowers that grow around the brim."

3.
"Be not in haste, young Nancy," this young man he did say,
"And I will bear you company and guard you on the way,
I live on yonder river-side where fishes they do swim,
Where you may gather flowers that grow around the brim."

4.
"Kind Sir, you must excuse me," this maiden did reply,
"I will not walk with any man until the day I die;
I have a sweetheart of my own, and him my heart has won:
He lived in yonder cottage, a wealthy farmer's son."

5.
"And pray what is your lover's name?" he unto her did say,
"Though in my tarry trousers, perhaps I know him may."
She said "His name is William, from that I'll never run;
This ring we broke at parting. He's a wealthy farmer's son."

6.
The ring out of his pocket he instantly then drew,
Saying "Nancy, here's the parting gift; one half I left with you.
I have been pressed to sea, and many a battle won;
But still your heart could ne'er depart from me, the farmer's son."

7.
When these words she heard him say, it put her in surprise,
The tear-drops they came trinkling down from her sparkling eyes.
"Oh, soothe your grief!" the young man cried, "the battle you have won,
For Hymen's chains shall bind us—you, and the farmer's son."

8.
To church, then, went this couple, and married were with speed.
The village bells they all did ring, and the girls did dance indeed.
She blessed the happy hour she in the fields did run,
To seek all for her true love, the wealthy farmer's son.

[Sung by Mr H. Burstow, 1893]

The Merchant's Daughter
or
The Constant Farmer's Son.

[SUSSEX]

Moderato.

It's of a merchant's daughter in London town did dwell So modest, fair and handsome; her parents loved her well. She was admired by lord and squire, but all their thoughts were vain, For only one,... A farmer's son, young Mary's heart did gain.

H.5873.

1.

It's of a merchant's daughter in London town did dwell,
So modest, fair and handsome, her parents loved her well.
She was admired by lord and squire, but all their thoughts were vain,
For only one, a farmer's son, young Mary's heart did gain.

2.

Long time young William courted her, and fixed their wedding day,
Their parents all consented, but her brothers both did say
"There lives a lord who pledged his word, and him she shall not shun;
We will betray and then we'll slay her constant farmer's son."

3.

A fair was held not far from town; these brothers went straightway,
And asked young William's company with them to pass the day;
But mark— returning home again they swore his race was run,
Then, with a stake, the life did take of her constant farmer's son.

4.

These villains then returning home "O sister," they did say,
"Pray think no more of your false love, but let him go his way,
For it's truth we tell, in love he fell, and with some other one;
Therefore we come to tell the same of the constant farmer's son."

5.

As on her pillow Mary lay, she had a dreadful dream,
She dreamt she saw his body lay down by a crystal stream,
Then she arose, put on her clothes, to seek her love did run,
When dead, and cold, she did behold her constant farmer's son.

6.

The salt tear stood upon his cheeks, all mingled with his gore,
She shrieked in vain, to ease her pain, and kiss'd him ten times o'er,
She gathered green leaves from the trees, to keep him from the sun,
One night and day she passed away with the constant farmer's son.

7.

But hunger it came creeping on; poor girl she shrieked with woe;
To try and find his murderer she straightway home did go,
Saying "Parents dear, you soon shall hear, a dreadful deed is done,
In yonder vale lies, dead and pale, my constant farmer's son."

8.

Up came her eldest brother and said "It is not me,"
The same replied the younger one, and swore most bitterly,
But young Mary said "Don't turn so red, nor try the laws to shun,
You've done the deed, and you shall bleed for my constant farmer's son!"

9.

Those villains soon they owned their guilt, and for the same did die;
Young Mary fair, in deep despair, she never ceased to cry;
The parents they did fade away, the glass of life was run,
And Mary cried, in sorrow died for her constant farmer's son.

[*Sung by M*ʳ *H. Burstow, 1893*]

Henry Martin
or Salt Seas.

[SUSSEX.]

Allegro con spirito.

1. There were three brothers in merry Scotland, In merry Scotland lived these...... And they did cast lots one with the other, o—ther, To know who should rob the salt seas......

2. The lot it fell on Henry Martin the youngest of the three To go a Scotch robbing all on the salt sea, salt sea To maintain his two brothers and he......

1.
There were three brothers in merry Scotland,
In merry Scotland lived these,
And they did cast lots, one with the other, other,
To know who should rob the salt seas.

2.
The lot it fell on Henry Martin,
The youngest of the three,
To go a Scotch-robbing all on the salt sea, salt sea,
To maintain his two brothers and he.

3.
They had not sailed three cold winter's nights,
Nor scarcely cold winter's nights three,
Before they espied a lofty tall ship, tall ship,
Come sailing all on the salt sea.

4.
"Where are you going?" said Henry Martin,
"How dare you sail so nigh?"
"I'm a rich merchant's ship to fair England bound, England bound,
So I pray you to let me pass {free!'/by.}

5.
"Oh, no! oh, no!" cried Henry Martin
"Such a thing as that never can be,
For I'm a Scotch robber, all on the salt sea, salt sea,
To maintain my two brothers and me!"

6.
So broadside to broadside in battle they went,
They fought full two hours or three,
Till Henry Martin gave her her death wound, death wound,
And down to the bottom sank she.

7.
Bad news, bad news, my brave Englishmen,
Bad news I now bring to town:
The rich merchant's ship she is now cast away, cast away,
And the most of her merry men did drown.

[*Sung by Mr H. Burstow, 1893.*]

Georgie
or Banstead Downs.

[SUSSEX.]

Moderato.

p legato

1. As I rode o-ver Banstead Downs, One mid-May morning ear-ly, There I es-pied a pret-ty fair maid La-ment-ing for her Georgie.

2. Say-ing "Georgie never stood on the King's highway, He ne-ver rob-bèd mo-ney, But he stole fif-teen of the King's fat deer, And sent them to Lord Na-vey."

H.5873.

1.
As I rode over Banstead Downs,
One mid-May morning early,
There I espied a pretty fair maid
Lamenting for her Georgie.

2.
Saying "Georgie never stood on the King's highway
He never robbèd money,
But he stole fifteen of the King's fat deer,
And sent them to Lord Navey.

3.
Oh, come and saddle my milk-white steed,
And bridle it all ready,
That I may go to my good Lord Judge
And ask the life of my Georgie."

4.
And when she came to the good Lord Judge
She fell down upon her knees already,
Saying "My good Lord Judge, come pity me,
Grant me the life of my Georgie."

5.
The Judge looked over his left shoulder,
He seemed as he was very sorry:
"My pretty fair maid, you are come too late,
For he is condemned already.

6.
He will be hung in a silken cord
Where there has not been many,
For he came of royal blood,
And courted a virtuous lady."

7.
"I wish I was on yonder hill,
Where times I have been many!
With a sword and buckler by my side
I would fight for the life of my Georgie."

[*Sung by Mr H. Burstow, 1893.*]

34

Boney's Lamentation.
[or Abdication.]

[SUSSEX.]

Pomposo e ben marcato.

At-tend, you sons of...... high re-nown, To these few lines which I pen down: I was born to wear a state-ly crown, And to rule a weal-thy na-tion. I am the man that beat Beau-lieu, And Wurm-ser's will did then sub-due; That great Arch-duke I

H.5873.

o-ver-threw; On ev-'ry plain my men were slain. Grand trea-sures, too, I did ob-tain, And got ca-pi-tu-la-tion.

after last verse.

1.
Attend, you sons of high renown,
To these few lines which I pen down:
I was born to wear a stately crown,
 And to rule a wealthy nation.
I am the man that beat Beaulieu,
And Wurmser's will did then subdue;
That great Archduke I overthrew.
 On every plain
 My men were slain.
Grand treasures, too, I did obtain,
 And got capitulation.

2.
I did pursue the Egyptians sore,
Till Turks and Arabs lay in gore;
The rights of France I did restore
 So long in confiscation.
I chased my foes through mud and mire
Till in despair my men did tire.
Then Moscow town was set on fire,
 My men were lost
 Through winter frost;
I ne'er before received such blast
 Since the hour of my creation.

3.
To Leipsic town my soldiers fled,
Montmartre was strewed with Prussian dead,
We marched {them/men} forth, inveterate,
 To stop a bold invasion.
Farewell, my royal spouse, once more,
And offspring great, whom I adore!
And may you that great throne restore,
 That is torn away,
 Without delay!
Those kings of me have made a prey,
 And caused my {lamentation./abdication.}

See Appendix page 117.   [*Sung by Mr H. Burstow, 1893.*]   H.5873.

Belfast Mountains.

Andante espressivo.
sempre legato

[SUSSEX.]

1. All on {those/the} Belfast mountains I heard a maid complain, Making forth her lamentation down by {some/a} purling stream, Saying "My heart is fettered, fast in the bonds of love, All by a false pretender who doth inconstant prove.

H.5873.

1.

All on {those/the} Belfast Mountains I heard a maid complain,
Making forth her lamentation down by {some/a} purling stream.
Saying "My heart is fettered, fast in the bonds of love,
All by a false pretender who doth inconstant prove.

2.

Oh, Johnny! my dear jewel, don't treat me with disdain!
Nor leave me here behind you in sorrow to complain!"
With her arms she clasps around him, like violets round the vine,
Saying "My bonny Cheshire lad, you've stole this heart of mine."

3.

Omit when singing.
["My dear, I'm sorry for you, that you for me should grieve,
I am engaged already; 'tis you I can't relieve."
"Since it is so, my Johnny, for ever I'm undone,
All by this shame and scandal I shall distracted run.

4.

If I'd but all those diamonds on yonder rock that grow
I would give them to my Cheshire lad if his love to me he'd show."
Wringing her hands and crying "My Johnny dear, farewell!
Unto those Belfast Mountains my sorrow I will tell.

5.

It's not those Belfast Mountains can give to me relief,
Nor is it in their power to ease me of my grief;
If they'd but a tongue to prattle to tell my love a tale,
Unto my bonny Cheshire lad my mind they would reveal."

[*Sung by M! H. Burstow, 1893.*]

See Appendix page 118.

The Young Servant Man.
or
The Two Affectionate Lovers.

[SUSSEX]

Allegro con spirito.

It's of a damsel both fair and handsome, (These lines are true, as I've been told.) Near the banks of Shannon, in a lofty mansion, Her father garner'd great stores of gold. Her hair was black as a raven's feather, Her form and features oh! describe who can? But still, it's a folly belongs to Nature: She fell in love with a servant man.

1.

It's of a damsel both fair and handsome,
These lines are true, as I've been told.
Near the banks of Shannon, in a lofty mansion,
Her father garnered great stores of gold.
Her hair was black as a raven's feather,
Her form and features oh! describe who can?
But still, it's a folly belongs to Nature:
She fell in love with a servant-man.

2.

As those two lovers were fondly talking,
Her father heard them, and near them drew;
As those two lovers were fondly talking,
In anger home her father flew;
To build a dungeon was his intention,
To part true love he contrived a plan,
He swore an oath by all his mansion
He'd part that fair one from her servant-man.

3.

So he built a dungeon with bricks and mortar,
With a flight of steps, for it was underground;
The food he gave her was bread and water,
The only comfort for her was found.
Three times a day he cruelly beat her,
Unto her father she thus began:
"If I've transgressed, my own dear father,
I will lie and die for my servant-man."

4.

Young Edwin found her habitation,
It was secured by an iron door.
He vowed, in spite of all the nation
He would gain her freedom, or rest no more.
So, at his leisure, he toiled with pleasure
To gain the freedom of Mary Ann;
And when he had found out his treasure
She cried "My faithful young servant-man!"

5.

Said Edwin "Now I've found my treasure
I will be true to you likewise,
And for your sake I will face your father;
To see me here it will him surprise."
When her father brought her bread and water
To call his daughter he then began,
Said Edwin "Enter, I've freed your daughter,
I will suffer — your servant-man!"

6.

When her father found that she was vanished,
Then like a lion he thus did roar,
Saying, "From Ireland you shall be banished,
And with my sword I will spill your gore!"
"Agreed," said Edwin, "I freed your daughter,
I freed your daughter, do all you can;
But forgive your treasure, I'll die with pleasure,
For the one in fault is your servant-man."

7.

When her father found him so tender-hearted,
Then down he fell on the dungeon floor,
Saying that love should never be parted,
Since love can enter an iron door.
So soon they're one, to be parted never,
And roll in riches this young couple can,
This fair young lady is blessed with pleasure,
Contented with her young servant-man.

[*Sung by Mr. Walter Searle, 1901.*]

See Appendix page 118.

Death and the Lady.

[SUSSEX.]

Andante non troppo lento.

1. *(Death)* "Fair lady, throw those costly robes aside. No longer may you glory in your pride. Take leave of all your carnal vain delight; I'm come to summon you away this night."

2. *(Lady)* *poco più mosso e agitato* "What bold attempt is this? pray let me know From whence you come, and whither I must go. Shall I, who am a lady, stoop or bow To such a pale-faced visage? Who art thou?"

3. *(D)* "Do die.

+ sometimes 'lay'.

H. 5873.

DEATH   **1.**
"Fair Lady, throw those costly robes aside,
No longer may you glory in your pride;
Take leave of all your carnal vain delight,
I'm come to summon you away this night."

LADY.   **2.**
"What bold attempt is this? Pray let me know
From whence you come, and whither I must go.
Shall I, who am a lady, stoop or bow
To such a pale-faced visage? Who art thou?"

3.
D. "Do you not know me? I will tell you then:
I am he that conquers all the sons of men,
No pitch of honour from my dart is free,
My name is Death! Have you not heard of me?"

4.
L. "Yes; I have heard of thee, time after time;
But, being in the glory of my prime,
I did not think you would have come so soon;
Why must my morning sun go down at noon?"

5.
D. "Talk not of noon! you may as well be mute;
There is no time at all for vain dispute,
Your riches, gold, and garments, jewels bright,
Your house, and land, must on new owners light."

6.
L. "My heart is cold; it trembles at such news!
{There's} bags of gold, if you will me excuse
{Here's}
And seize on those; and finish thou *their* strife,
Who wretched are, and weary of their life.

7.
Are there not many bound in prison strong
In bitter grief? and souls that languish long,
Who could but find the grave a place of rest
From all their grief, by which they are opprest.

8.
Besides there's many with a hoary head
And palsied joints; from whom all joy is fled.
Release thou them whose sorrows are so great,
And spare my life until a later date!"

9.
D. "Though thy vain heart to riches is inclined
Yet thou must die and leave them all behind.
I come to none before their warrant's sealed,
And, when it is, they must submit, and yield.

10.
Though some by age be full of grief and pain,
Till their appointed time they must remain;
I take no bribe, believe me, this is true.
Prepare yourself to go; I'm come for you."

11.
L. "But if, oh! if you could for me obtain
A freedom, and a longer life to reign,
Fain would I stay, if thou my life wouldst spare.
I have a daughter, beautiful and fair,
{I wish to see her wed, whom I adore;
✢{Grant me but this, and I will ask no more."

12.
D. "This is a slender frivolous excuse!
I have you fast! I will not let you loose!
Leave her to Providence, for you must go
Along with me, whether you will or no!

13.
If Death commands the King to leave his crown
He at my feet must lay his sceptre down;
Then, if to *Kings* I do not favour give
But cut them off, can *you* expect to live
{Beyond the limits of your time and space?
✢{No! I must send you to another place."

14.
L. "Ye learned doctors, now exert your skill,
And let not Death on me obtain his will!
Prepare your cordials, let me comfort find,
My gold shall fly like chaff before the wind!"

15.
D. "Forbear to call! that skill will never do;
They are but mortals here as well as you.
I give the fatal wound, my dart is sure,
And far beyond the doctors' skill to cure.

16.
How freely you can let your riches fly
To purchase life, rather than yield and die!
But, while you flourished here with all your store,
You would not give one penny to the poor.

17.
Though in God's name they sue to you did make
You would not spare one penny for His sake.
My Lord beheld wherein you did amiss,
And calls you hence, to give account of this."

18.
L. "Oh! heavy news! must I no longer stay?
How shall I stand at the great Judgement Day?"
Down from her eyes the crystal tears did flow,
She says "None knows what I now undergo!

19.
Upon my bed of sorrow here I lie!
My selfish life makes me afraid to die!
My sins are great, and manifold, and foul;
Lord Jesus Christ have mercy on my soul!

20.
Alas! I do deserve a righteous frown!
Yet pardon, Lord, and pour a blessing down!"
Then with a dying sigh her heart did break,
And did the pleasures of this world forsake.

21.
Thus may we see the mighty rise and fall,
For cruel Death shews no respect at all
To those of either high or low degree.
The great submit to Death as well as we.

22.
Though they are gay, their life is but a span,
A lump of clay, so vile a creature's Man!
Then happy they whom God hath made his care,
And die in God, and ever happy are!

23.
The grave's the market place where all must meet
Both rich and poor, as well as small and great;
If life were merchandise, that gold could buy,
The rich would live—only the poor would die.

*Occasionally 'lay' for 'throw.'   [*Sung by Mr H. Burstow, 1893.*]   ✢ Repeat last part of tune.

See Appendix page **118**.   H.5873.

The Three Butchers.
or
Gibson, Wilson and Johnson.

[SUSSEX.]

Allegro con spirito.

1. A story I will tell to you, it is of butchers three: Gibson, Wilson, and Johnson, mark well what I do say; Now as they had five hundred pounds, all on a market day, Now as they had five hundred pounds to pay upon their way, With my

3. "Oh woman, woman," Johnson cries, "Oh pray, come tell to me, Oh woman, woman" Johnson cries, "Have you got any company?" "Oh, no! no! no!" the woman cries, "Alas! how can that be, When here have been by ten swaggering blades who've robbed and beaten me? With my

H. 5873.

hey ding ding, With my ho, ding ding, With my high ding ding, high dey......... +May
hey ding ding, With my ho, ding ding, With my high ding ding, high dey......... May

God keep all..... good peo_ple from such bad com_pa_ny!
God keep all..... good peo_ple from such bad com_pa_ny!

2. Now as they rode a_long the...road as fast as they could {ride.} "Spur
4. Now John_son, be_ing a va_liant man, he bore a va_liant mind,   He

on your horse" says John_son "for I hear a wo_man cry!" And
wropped her up in his great coat, And placed her up be_hind. And

as they rode in_to..... the wood the scene they {spied / scanned} a_round,..... And
as they rode a_long the road as fast as they could ride,....... She

+*or* 'May Heaven keep good people.'

there they found a woman lay a-swooning on the ground. *With my*
put her fingers to her ear and gave a screekful cry. *With my*

hey, ding, ding, with my ho, ding, ding, With my high ding ding, high dey!...... May
hey, ding, ding, with my ho, ding, ding, With my high ding ding, high dey!...... May

gves ad libitum.

God keep all.... good peo - ple from such bad com - pa - ny!
God keep all.... good peo - ple from such bad com - pa - ny!

5. "With that came out ten swaggering blades with their rapiers {ready drawn, in their hand,} They rode up to bold
7. "Come on, come on!" cries bold John-son, "there are but five for me, And, woman, stand you

John-son, and bold-ly bid him stand. "Oh, I can not fight," says Gib-son, "I am
here behind; we'll gain the vic-to-ry!" The very next pis-tol Johnson fired was

H. 5873.

sure that I shall die!"...."No more won't I"cries Wil_son "For I will sooner
loaded with powder and ball..... And out of these five swaggering blades there's three of them did

fly!" With my hey, ding, ding, With my ho, ding, ding, With my high ding, ding, high
fall. With my hey, ding, ding, With my ho, ding, ding, With my high ding, ding, high

dey!......... May God keep all good peo_ple from such bad com_pa_ny!
dey!......... May God keep all good peo_ple from such bad com_pa_ny!

6 "Come on! come on!" cries bold Johnson "I'll fight you all so free! And woman, stand you
8. "Come on! come on!" cries bold Johnson "there are but two to me! And woman, stand you

here be_hind; we'll gain the vic_to_ry!" The ve_ry next pis_tol
here be_hind; we'll gain the vic_to_ry!" As John_son fought those

46

Johnson fires was loaded with powder and ball,.... And out of these ten swaggering blades five of them did fall. *With my hey, ding, ding, With my ho, ding, ding, With my high ding ding, high dey!........ May God keep all good peo_ple from such bad com_pa_ny!*

rogues in front the woman he did not mind,.. She took his knife all from his side, and stabbed him from be_hind. *With my hey, ding, ding, With my ho, ding, ding, With my high ding ding, high dey!........ May God keep all good peo_ple from such bad com_pa_ny!*

8ves ad libitum.

9. "Now I must fall", says John_son "I must fall to the ground! For re_liev_ing this wick_ed wo_man she.... gave me my death wound! Oh!

H. 5873.

woman, wo_man, wo_ _ man, what have you been and done?......... You have killed the fi_nest butch _ er that ev_er the sun shone on!" *With my hey ding ding, with my ho ding ding, With my high ding ding, high dey......... May God keep all..... good peo _ ple from such bad com _ pa _ ny!*

10. Now, just as she had done the deed some men came ri_ding by, And

48

see-ing what this wo-man had done, they raised a dreadful cry. Then she was condemned to die in links and i-ron chains so strong, For killing of bold John-son, that great and valiant man. *With my hey, ding, ding, with my ho, ding, ding, With my high ding ding, high dey!* May God keep all good peo-ple from such bad com-pa-ny!

8ves. ad libitum.

H.5873.

1.

A story I will tell to you, it is of butchers three:
Gibson, Wilson and Johnson, mark well what I do say;
Now as they had five hundred pounds, all on a market day,
Now as they had five hundred pounds to pay upon their way.
With my hey, ding, ding, with my ho, ding, ding,
With my high, ding, ding, high dey!
†*May God keep all good people from such bad company!*

2.

Now as they rode along the road as fast as they could {ride, / hie,}
"Spur on your horse," says Johnson, "for I hear a woman cry,"
And, as they rode into the wood, the scene they spied around,
And there they found a woman lay a-swooning on the ground.
With etc:

3.

"O woman, woman," Johnson cries, "oh pray, come tell to me,
O woman, woman," Johnson cries, "have you got any company?"
"Oh, no! no! no!" the woman cries, "Alas! how can that be?
When here have been by ten swaggering blades who've robbed and beaten me!"
With etc:

4.

Now Johnson, being a valiant man, he bore a valiant mind,
He wropped her up in his great coat, and placed her up behind.
And as they rode along the road, as fast as they could ride,
She put her fingers to her ear and gave a screekful cry.
With etc:

5.

With that, came out ten swaggering blades, with their rapiers {ready drawn, / in their hand.}
They rode up to bold Johnson, and boldly bid him stand.
"Oh, I cannot fight," says Gibson, "I am sure that I shall die!"
"No more won't I," cries Wilson, "for I will sooner fly!"
With etc:

6.

"Come on, come on!" cries bold Johnson, "I'll fight you all so free!
And, woman, stand you here behind; we'll gain the victory!"
The very first pistol Johnson fires was loaded with powder and ball,
And, out of these ten swaggering blades five of them did fall.
With etc:

7.

"Come on! come on!" cries bold Johnson, "there are but five for me,
And, woman, stand you there behind; we'll gain the victory!"
The very next pistol Johnson fired was loaded with powder and ball,
And out of these five swaggering blades there's three of them did fall.
With etc:

8.

"Come on! come on!" cries bold Johnson, "there are but two to me,
And, woman, stand you there behind; we'll gain the victory!"
As Johnson fought these rogues in front, the woman he did not mind,
She took his knife all from his side {and ripped him down behind. / and stabbed him from behind.}
With etc:

9.

"Now I must fall," says Johnson, "I must fall to the ground!
For relieving this wicked woman she gave me my death wound!
Oh! woman, woman, woman, what have you been and done?
You have killed the finest butcher that ever the sun shone on!"
With etc:

10.

Now, just as she had done the deed some men came riding by,
And, seeing what this woman had done, they raised a dreadful cry.
Then she was condemned to die in links, and iron chains so strong,
For killing of bold Johnson, that great and valiant man.
With etc:

[*Sung by Mr H. Burstow, 1893.*]

See Appendix page 119.   †or "May Heaven keep good people"

I.
The Unquiet Grave
or
How cold the Winds do blow.

[SURREY.]

Andante espressivo.

sempre legato e **pp**

"How cold the winds do blow, dear love! And a few small drops of rain! I

pp

Verses 1-6.

ne_ver, ne_ver had but one true love; In the greenwood he was slain......... 2 I'll

Last verse.

all must die When Christ calls us... a _ way."

molto **pp** *e legato*   *dim.*   *rit.*   **ppp**

H.5873.

1.

"How cold the winds do blow, dear love!
And a few small drops of rain!
I never, never had but one true love;
In the greenwood he was slain.

2.

I'll do as much for my true love
As any young girl may:
I'll sit and mourn upon his grave
For a twelvemonth and a day."

3.

When twelve months and a day were up
Then he began to speak
Saying "Who is that, sits upon my grave,
And will not let me sleep?"

4.

"It's I, it's I, your own true love,
Your own true love!" said she,
"One single sweet kiss from your clay-cold lips!
That's all I want from thee!"

5.

"My lips they are as cold as clay
My breath is earthy and strong,
And if you were to kiss my clay-cold lips
Your life would not be long.

6.

It's down in yonder garden, love,
Where you and I used to walk,
There's finest flowers that ever grew
That's withered to the stalk.

7.

They're withered and dried up, dear love,
Never to return any day,
So it's you, and I, and all must die
When Christ calls us away."

The two beautiful stanzas on page 55, which end Mrs. Jeffreys' version, may be used as an ending to the above.

[*Sung by Mr James Bromham, 1896*]

II.
The Unquiet Grave
or
How cold the Winds do blow.

[SURREY.]

Andante espressivo.

"How cold the winds do blow, dear love! And a few small drops of...... rain, I ne_ver ne_ver had but one true love, In the greenwood he was slain............ I'll

Verses 1-6.

Last verse.

Christ calls us a _ way."

H.5873.

1.

"How cold the winds do blow, dear love!
And a few small drops of rain!
I never, never had but one true love,
In the greenwood he was slain.

2.

I'll do as much for my true love
As any young girl may:
I'll sit and mourn upon his grave
For twelve months and a day."

3.

When twelve months and a day were up
Then he began to speak
"O, who is it sits upon my grave
And will not let me sleep?"

4.

"It's I, it's I, your own true love,
Your own true love!" said she
"One single sweet kiss from your clay-cold lips!
That's all I want from thee!"

5.

"My lips they are as cold as [any] clay,
My breath is heavy and strong,
If you were to kiss my clay-cold lips
Your life it won't be long.

6.

It's down in yonder garden, love,
Where we were used to walk,
There's finest flowers that ever grew
All withered to the stalk.

7.

They're withered and dried up, dear love,
Never to return any day,
So it's you, and I, and all must die,
When Christ calls us away."

[Sung by Mrs. Rugman, 1896]

III.
The Unquiet Grave
or
Cold blows the Wind.

[N. DEVONSHIRE]

Andante espressivo.

legato

"Cold blows the wind o'er my true love, Cold blow the drops of.... rain, I never had but one true love, In greenwood he............ was slain........

dim.

H.5873.

1.

"Cold blows the wind o'er my true love,
 Cold blow the drops of rain,
 I never had but one true love,
 In the greenwood he was slain.

2.

I'll do as much for my true love
 As any young girl may:
 I'll sit and weep down by his grave
 For twelve months and a day."

3.

But when twelve months were come and gone
 This young man he arose:
"What makes you weep down by my grave?
 I can't take my repose."

4.

"One kiss, one kiss of your lily-white lips,
 One kiss is all I crave!
 One kiss, one kiss of your lily-white lips,
 And return back to your grave."

5.

"My lips they are as cold as clay,
 My breath is heavy and strong;
 If thou wast to kiss my lily-white lips,
 Thy days would not be long!

6.

O don't you remember the garden grove
 Where we was used to walk?
 Pluck the finest flower of them all,
 'Twill wither to a stalk."

7.

"My time be long, my time be short,
 To-morrow or to-day,
 Sweet Christ in heaven will have my soul,
 And take my life away."

8.

"Don't grieve, don't grieve for me, true love,
 No mourning do I crave;
 I must leave you and all the world,
 And sink down in my grave."

[Sung by Mrs. Jeffreys, 1893.]

Oh, the Trees are getting high.

[SURREY.]

Lento e espressivo.

"Oh! the trees are get_ting high.... and the leaves are growing green; The time is gone and past, my love, that you and I have seen! 'Twas on a win_ter's eve_ning, as I sat all a_lone, There I spied a bon_ny boy, young, but grow_ing.

1.

"Oh! the trees are getting high, and the leaves are getting green;
The time is gone and past, my love, that you and I have seen!
'Twas on a winter's evening, as I sat all alone,
There I spied a bonny boy, young, but growing.

2.

Oh mother! dear mother! you've done to me much wrong!
You've married me to a bonny boy, his age it is so young!
His age is only twelve, and myself scarcely thirteen!"
Saying "My bonny boy is young, but a-growing."

3.

"It's daughter! dear daughter! I have done to you no wrong;
I have married you to a bonny boy, he is some rich lord's son,
And a lady he will make you, that's if you will be made,"
Saying "Your bonny boy is young, but a-growing."

4.

"Oh mother! dear mother! I'm but a child 'tis true,
I'll go back to my old college for another year or two;
I'll cut off my yellow hair, put my box upon my head,
And I'll gang along with it to the college."

5.

And at the age of thirteen he was a married man;
And at the age of fourteen he was father of a son;
And at the age of fifteen then his grave was growing green:
So there was an end to his growing.

[Sung by Mr Ede, 1896]

Our Ship she lies in Harbour.

[SURREY.]

Moderato.

sempre legato.

"Our ship she lies in harbour, Just ready to set sail, May heaven be your guardian, love, Till I return from sea."

1.
"Our ship she lies in harbour,
Just ready to set sail,
May heaven be your guardian, love,
Till I return from sea."

2.
Said the father to the daughter,
"What makes you so lament?
Is there no man in all the world
Could give your heart content?"

3.
Said the daughter to the father,
"I'll tell [you] the reason why:
You have sent away that sailor-lad
That could me satisfy."

4.
"If that's your inclination,"
The father did reply,
"I wish he may continue there,
And on the seas may die!"

5.
She, like an angel weeping,
On the rocks sighed every day,
Awaiting for her own true love
Returning home from sea.

6.
"Oh, yonder sits my angel!
She's waiting there for me,
To-morrow to the church we'll go,
And married we will be."

7.
When they had been to church, and were
Returning back again,
She espied her honoured father
And several gentlemen.

8.
Said the father to the daughter,
"Five hundred pounds I'll give,
If you'll forsake that sailor-lad
And come with me to live."

9.
"It's not your gold that glittered,
Nor yet your silver that shined,
For I'm married to the man I love
And I'm happy in my mind!"

[*Sung by Mr Sparks, 1896.*]

The Irish Girl.
or
The New Irish Girl.

[MIXOLYDIAN.] [SURREY.]

Allegro moderato.

1. Abroad as I was walking, down by the river side, I gazed all around.... me, an Irish girl I spied; So...... red and rosy were her cheeks and yellow was her hair, And
2. The very last time I saw my love she seem'd to lie in pain, With sorrow, grief and anguish her heart was broke in twain: "Oh there's many a man that's worse than he, then why should I..... complain? Oh!

H.5873.

cost - ly were the robes of gold my I - rish girl did
love is such a kill - ing thing! did you ev - er feel the

wear. 2. Her shoes were of the Span - ish black, all
pain?" 4. I wish my love was a red rose, and

span - gled
in the

span - gled round with dew, She wrung her hands, she
in the gar - den grew, And I to be the

tore her hair cry-ing "Love! what shall... I do? I'm....
gar - den - er; To her I would be true. There's

go - ing home! I'm go - ing home! I'm go - ing home!" said
not a month through - out the year, but love I would re -

she, "Why will you go a - ro - ving, and
- new; With li - lies I would gar - nish her, sweet

slight your dear Pol - lie?" 3. The wish I was a
Wil - li - am, thyme and rue. 5. I

but - ter - fly, I'd fly to my love's breast; I

wish I was a lin-net, I'd sing my love to rest; I wish I was a night-in-gale, I'd sing till morn-ing clear; I'd sit and sing to you Pol-lie, the girl I love so dear. 6. I

seat - - ed

wish I was at Ex_e_ter all seat_ed on the grass, With a bot_tle of whis_key in my hand, and on my knee a lass. I'd..... call for liquor mer_ri_ly, and... pay be_fore I go; I'd hold her in my arms once more, let the wind blow high or low.

1

Abroad as I was walking down by the river side,
I gazèd all around me, an Irish girl I spied;
So red and rosy were her cheeks, and yellow was her hair,
And costly were the robes of gold my Irish girl did wear.

2

Her shoes were of the Spanish black, all spangled round with dew,
She wrung her hands, and tore her hair, crying "Love! what shall I do?
I'm going home, I'm going home, I'm going home," said she,
"Why will you go a-roving, and slight your dear Polliè?"

3

The very last time I saw my love she seemed to lie in pain,
With sorrow, grief and anguish her heart was broke in twain:
"Oh! there's many a man that's worse than he, then why should I complain?
Oh! love is such a killing thing! did you ever feel the pain?"

4

I wish my love was a red rose, and in the garden grew,
And I to be the gardener; to her I would be true.
There's not a month throughout the year, but love I would renew:
With lilies I would garnish her, sweet William, thyme, and rue.

5

I wish I was a butterfly, I'd fly to my love's breast;
I wish I was a linnet, I'd sing my love to rest;
I wish I was a nightingale, I'd sing till morning clear,
I'd sit and sing to you, Pollie, the girl I love so dear.

6

may be omitted when singing.
⎡I wish I was at Exeter, all seated on the grass,
⎢With a bottle of whiskey in my hand, and on my knee a lass.
⎢I'd call for liquor merrily, and pay before I go;
⎣I'd hold her in my arms once more, let the wind blow high or low.

[*Sung by M*ͬ *James Bromham, 1896.*]

The Little Lowland Maid.

[SURREY.]

Allegro con spirito.

It's of a pretty sailor lad who ploughed the stormy sea, He dressed himself in tarry clothes, like one in poverty; His pockets being well lined, though of the sailor trade, For to try the heart of Mary Ann, the little Lowland Maid.

H. 5873.

1.

It's of a pretty sailor lad who ploughed the stormy sea,
He dressed himself in tarry clothes, like one in poverty;
His pockets being well linèd, though of the sailor trade,
For to try the heart of Mary Ann, the little Lowland Maid.

2.

As Mary Ann was standing down by her cottage door
She frowned upon her sailor lad, who seemed to be so poor.
She looked just like a goddess, in jewels rich arrayed,
But the thorn was in the bosom of the little Lowland Maid.

3.

"Good morning," said false Mary Ann, "I'm glad to meet with you;
Have you forgot your own true love, or changed your love for new?
Or is your inclination all on some other strayed?
So begone!" said lovely Mary Ann, the little Lowland Maid.

4.

She seemed to be so scornful, so the sailor says "Behold!"
All from his trousers-pocket he pulls a bag of gold.
So then replied false Mary Ann "Excuse me what I said!
You're welcome to the cottage and the little Lowland Maid."

5.

"Oh no! deceitful damsel, your falseness shall be paid,
For I can lie till morning in some distant barn or shed."
It was the hour of twelve o'clock young Mary Ann did stray,
And she told some other comrade where the sailor he did lay.

6.

They went with their dark lanterns and daggers in their hands,
They rode through woods and meadows, and past the muddy lands;
"Cheer up your hearts," said Mary Ann, "and do not be betrayed,
We will rob and slay the sailor for the little Lowland Maid."

7.

They both then plunged their daggers into the sailor, deep;
They robbed him of his glittering gold, and left him there to weep.
A gamekeeper was watching them; all from his wood he strayed,
Then he swore against the villain and the little Lowland Maid.

8.

They both then stood their trials, and were condemned, and cast;
And on the fatal gallows-tree they both were hung at last.
There were thousands flocked to see them, and scornfully they said
"Begone! you cruel monster, and the little Lowland Maid!"

[Sung by Mr Baker, 1896.]

See Appendix page 121.

The Rich Nobleman and his Daughter.

[SURREY.]

Allegro.

1. It's of a rich no_ble_man late_ly, we hear; He had but one daugh_ter, most beau_ti_ful, fair; And she was a_dor_èd, most beau_ti_ful child,... A bloom_ing young dam_sel that has me be_guiled.

1

It's of a rich nobleman lately, we hear;
He had but one daughter, most beautiful, fair;
And she was adorèd, most beautiful child,
A blooming young damsel that has me beguiled.

2

Her father being dead, and she at her ease,
To gaze on her work folks did ride in their chaise;
Till at length a young ploughboy came whistling by,
And on this young ploughboy she fixèd her eye.

3

Great raptures of love this young lady did show,
To gaze on his beauty to the fields she did go;
When he whistled so sweetly he made the groves ring,
And his cheeks were like roses that bloom in the Spring.

4

Then she and her maid, they agreed both to go
And dress themselves up in some regimental clothes,
With broad-sword in hand, they marched through the grove
To press this young ploughboy with a warrant of love.

5

Then, with this love letter she had in her hand:
"Here's an order for sea without more demand!
No cares, and no troubles, great bounty you'll take,
No danger on sea, you your fortune will make!"

6

Then in a close room this young man was confined
Till she changèd her dress; then she told him her mind.
Then she like an angel for beauty did appear,
And said "I'll prove true to thee, ploughboy so dear."

7

Now married this loving young couple they were,
In a sweet country life, and free from all care.
No cares and no troubles shall e'er them annoy,
They'll be happily blessed with a fountain of joy.

[*Sung by M⟨r⟩ Grantham, 1892.*]

70

The Poor Murdered Woman.

[DORIAN.] [SURREY.]

Allegro moderato.

1. It was Han-key the squi-èr, as I have heard say, Who rode out a-hunt-ing on one Sat-ur-day. They hunt-ed all day, but no-thing they found But a poor mur-dered wo-man, laid on the cold ground.

H.5873.

1

It was Hankey the squire, as I have heard say,
Who rode out a-hunting on one Saturday.
They hunted all day, but nothing they found
But a poor murdered woman, laid on the cold ground.

2

About eight o'clock, boys, our dogs they throwed off,
On Leatherhead Common, and that was the spot;
They tried all the bushes, but nothing they found
But a poor murdered woman, laid on the cold ground.

3

They whipped their dogs off, and kept them away,
For I do think it's proper he should have fair play;
They tried all the bushes, but nothing they found
But a poor murdered woman, laid on the cold ground.

4

They mounted their horses, and rode off the ground,
They rode to the village, and alarmed it all round,
"It is late in the evening, I am sorry to say,
She can not be removèd until the next day."

5

The next Sunday morning, about eight o'clock,
Some hundreds of people to the spot they did flock;
For to see the poor creature your hearts would have bled,
Some odious violence had come to her head.

6

She was took off the common, and down to some inn,
And the man that has kept it, his name is John Simms.
The coroner was sent for, the jury they joined,
And soon they concluded, and settled their mind.

7

Her coffin was brought; in it she was laid,
And took to the churchyard that was called Leatherhead,
No father, no mother, nor no friend, I'm told,
Come to see that poor creature put under the mould.

8

So now I'll conclude, and finish my song,
And those that have done it, they will find themselves wrong.
For the last day of Judgment the trumpet will sound,
And their souls not in heaven, I'm afraid, won't be found.

[*Sung by Mr Foster, 1897.*]

The Valiant Lady
or
The Brisk Young Lively Lad.

Allegro risoluto.

[SURREY.]

1. It's of a brisk young live-ly lad Came out of Gloucester-shire, And all his full in-ten-tion was To court a la-dy fair. Her eyes they shone like morn-ing dew, Her hair was fair too see; She was grace, In form and face, And was fixed in mo-des-ty

Verses 1-6.

H.5873.

1.
It's of a brisk young lively lad
   Came out of Gloucestershire,
And all his full intention was
   To court a lady fair.
Her eyes they shone like morning dew,
   Her hair was fair to see;
     She was grace,
     In form and face,
   And was fixed in modesty.

2.
This couple was a-walking,
   They loved each other well;
And someone heard them talking
   And did her father tell.
And when her father came to know
   And understand this thing,
     Then said he
     "From one like thee
   I'll free my daughter in the spring!"

3.
'Twas in the spring-time of the year
   There was a press begun;
And all their full intention was
   To press a farmer's son.
They pressèd him, and sent him out
   Far o'er the raging sea,
     "Where I'm sure
     He will no more
   Keep my daughter company!"

4.
In man's apparel then she did
   Resolve to try her fate;
And in the good ship where he rid
   She went as surgeon's mate.
Says she "My soldier shall not be
   Destroyed for want of care;
     I will dress,
     And I will bless,
   Whatsoever I endure!"

5.
The twenty-first of August
   There was a fight begun,
And foremost in the battle
   They placed the farmer's son.
He there received a dreadful wound
   That struck him in the thigh,
     Every vein
     Was filled with pain,
   He got wounded dreadfully.

6.
Into the surgeon's cabin
   They did convey him straight,
Where, first of all the wounded men,
   The pretty surgeon's mate
Most tenderly did dress his wound,
   Which bitterly did smart;
     Then said he
     "Oh! one like thee
   Once was mistress of my heart!"

7.
She went to the commander
   And offered very fair:
"Forty or fifty guineas
   Shall buy my love quite clear!
No money shall be wanted,
   No longer tarry here!"
     "Since 'tis so
     Come, let's go!
   To old England we will steer!"

8.
She went unto her father's gate
   And stood there for a while;
Said he "The heavens bless you!
   My own and lovely child!"
Cried she "Since I have found him,
   And brought him safe to shore,
     Our days we'll spend
     In old England,
   Never roam abroad no more!"

[Sung by Mr Baker, 1896.]

See Appendix page 121.

King Pharaoh.
[Gypsy Christmas Carol.]

[SUSSEX & SURREY.]

Andante.

legato

dolce

1. King... Pharaoh... sat a mu - sing, a - mu - sing all a...... lone; There came {a/the} bles - sed.... Sa - - viour, And all to him un - known.

H.5873.

[Original version.]	[Restored version.]

1.

King Pharim sat a-musing,	King Pharaoh sat a-musing,
A musing all alone;	A-musing all alone;
There came a blessed Saviour,	There came the blessed Saviour,
And all to him unknown.	And all to him unknown.

2.

"Say, where did you come from, good man,	"Say, where did you come from, good man?
Oh, where did you then pass?"	Oh, where did you then pass?"
"It is out of the land Egypt,	"It is out of the land of Egypt,
Between an ox and an ass."	Between an ox and ass."

3.

"Oh, if you come out of Egypt, man,	"Oh, if you come out of Egypt, man,
One thing I fain I known,	One thing I ween thou knowst:
Whether a blessed Virgin Mary	Is Jesus sprung of Mary
Sprung from an Holy Ghost?	And of the Holy Ghost?

4.

For if this is true, is true, good man,	For if this is true, is true, good man,
That you've been telling to me,	That you have told to me,
That the roasted cock do crow three times	Make this roasted cock to crow three times
In the place where they did stand."	In the dish that here we see!"

5.

Oh, it's straight away the cock did fetch,	Oh, it's straight away the cock did rise,
And feathered to your own hand,	All feathered to the hand,
Three times a roasted cock did crow,	Three times the roasted cock did crow,
On the place where they did stand.	On the place where they did stand.

6.

Joseph, Jesus and Mary	Joseph, Jesus and Mary
Were travelling for the west,	Were travelling for the west,
When Mary grew a-tired	When Mary grew a-tired
She might sit down and rest.	She might sit down and rest.

7.

They travelled further and further,	They travelled further and further,
The weather being so warm,	The weather being so warm,
Till they came unto some husbandman	Till they came unto a husbandman
A-sowing of his corn.	A-sowing of his corn.

8.

"Come husbandman!" cried Jesus,	"Come husbandman!" cried Jesus,
"From over speed and pride,	Throw all your seed {away, / aside,}
And carry home your ripened corn	And carry home as ripened corn
That you've been sowing this day.	That you have sowed this {day; / tide;}

9.

For to keep your wife and family	For to keep your wife and family
From sorrow, grief and pain,	From sorrow, grief and pain,
And keep Christ in your remembrance	And keep Christ in remembrance
Till the time comes round again."	{Till the time comes round again. / Till seed-time comes again.}

[Sung by Gypsies of the name of Goby. 1893]

See Appendix page 122.

The Moon shines bright.

[Christmas Carol.]

[SUSSEX & SURREY.]

Andante.

legatissimo e dolce

dolce

Oh, the moon shines bright, and the stars give a light; Oh, a little before the day, Our Lord, our God, He calls up-on us all, And He bids us a-wake and pray.

1

Oh the moon shines bright, and the stars give a light;
Oh, a little before the day,
Our Lord, our God, He calls upon us all,
And He bids us awake and pray.

2

Awake, awake, good people all,
Awake, and you shall hear:
Our blessed Saviour died upon the cross,
Saying Christ loved us so dear.

3

So dear, so dear Christ lovèd us,
And for our sins got slain;
We'll all leave off our wicked, wicked way,
And turn to the Lord again.

4

Oh, the life of man it is but a span,
He flourishes like a flower,
He's here to-day, and tomorrow he's gone,
And he's dead all in an hour.

5

Oh, teach your children well, good man,
As long as here you stay,
For it might be better for your sweet soul,
When your body lies under the clay.

6

There's a green turf at your head, good man,
And another at your feet.
*God bless you all, both great and small,
And I hope you a happy New Year.

[*Sung by Gypsies of the name of Goby, well known in Sussex & Surrey.*]

**Some versions have:*
   Your good deeds and your evil
   Will all together meet.

The Hampshire Mummers' Christmas Carol.

Andante.

There is six good days all in the week, All for a labouring man, But the seventh is the Sabbath of our Lord Jesus Christ, The Father and the Son.

1.

There is six good days all in the week,
All for a labouring man,
But the seventh is the Sabbath of our Lord Jesus Christ,
The Father and the Son.

2.

On Sunday go to church, dear man;
Down on our knees we must fall,
And then we must pray that the Lord Jesus Christ
He will bless and save us all.

3.

Bring up your children well, dear man,
Whilst they are in their youth,
For it might be the better for your sweet soul
When you go to the Lord {Jesus Christ. / of Truth.

4.

Now the fields they are as green, as green,
As green as any leaf,
Our Lord our God He has watered them
With the heavenly dew so sweet.

5.

In hell it is dark, in hell it is dim,
In hell it is full of lies;
And that is the place where all wicked men must go
When they part from the Lord Jesus Christ.

6.

Then take your Bible in your hand
And read your chapter through;
And when the day of Judgment comes,
The Lord remember you.

7.

Then bring us some of your Christmas ale,
And likewise your Christmas beer;
For when another Christmas comes
We may not all be here.

8.

With one stone at your head, oh man,
And another stone at your feet.
[Your good deeds and your evil
Will all together meet.]

[*Sung by Mummers of Kingsclere, 1897.*]

The Sussex Mummers' Christmas Carol.

Andante.

*1. When righteous Joseph wedded was Unto a †virtuous maid; A glorious angel from Heaven came, Unto that virtuous maid, Unto that †virtuous maid.

2. O mortal man, remember well When Christ our Lord was born, He was crucified betwixt two thieves And crowned with the thorn, And crowned with the thorn.

※ or verse 2 on to 3.

† or Virgin.

*Verse 1 does not appear in all versions, and may be omitted if the Carol is shortened.
The Mummers repeated the last half of each verse in Chorus.

H.5873.

3. O mortal man, remember well When
4. O mortal man, remember well When

Christ died on the rood; 'Twas for our sins and
Christ was wrapt in clay, He was taken to a

wicked ways Christ shed His precious blood, Christ
sepulchre Where no man ever lay, Where

shed His precious blood.
no man ever lay.

5. God

mf un poco animato

5. bless the mis_tress of this house With gold {chain/all} round her......
6. bless the mas_ter of this house With hap_pi_ness be_
7. bless your house, your chil_dren too, Your cat_tle and your

8ves. in basso ad libitum throughout verses 6 & 7.
and substitute f & ff for p & pp.

breast; Where_e'er her bo_dy sleeps or.... wakes, Lord,
_side; Where_e'er his bo_dy rides or.... walks, Lord
store; The Lord in_crease you day by.... day, And

cresc. *p*

send her soul to rest,............ Lord send............ her....
Je_sus be his guide,............ Lord Je_ _ sus...
give you more and more,............ and give............ you...

pp

| Verses 5 & 6. | Last verse
soul............ to rest. | 6. God..... more!
be............ his guide. | 7. God.....
more,............ and

H.5873.

1

When righteous Joseph wedded was
Unto a {virtuous/virgin} maid,
A glorious angel from Heaven came
Unto that {virtuous/virgin} maid.

Omit when fewer verses are desired.

2

O mortal man, remember well
When Christ our Lord was born;
He was crucified betwixt two thieves,
And crownèd with the thorn.

3

O mortal man, remember well
When Christ died on the rood,
'Twas for our sins and wicked ways
Christ shed His precious blood.

4

O mortal man, remember well
When Christ was wrapped in clay,
He was taken to a sepulchre
Where no man ever lay.

5

God bless the mistress of this house
With gold {all/chain} round her breast;
*Where e'er her body sleeps or wakes,
Lord, send her soul to rest.

6

God bless the master of this house
With happiness beside;
Where e'er his body rides or walks
Lord Jesus be his guide.

7

God bless your house, your children too,
Your cattle and your store;
The Lord increase you day by day,
And {send/give} you more and more.

[*Sung by Mummers from the neighbourhood of Horsham about 1878 – 1881.*]

*"*Wherever she sleeps or where she weeps*" *in another version.*

Bedfordshire May Day Carol.

Allegretto.

1. I've been rambling all the night, And the best part of the day; And now I am returning back again, I have brought you a branch of May.

1

I've been rambling all the night,
  And the best part of the day;
And now I am returning back again,
  I have brought you a branch of May.

2

A branch of May, my dear, I say,
  Before your door I stand,
It's nothing but a sprout, but it's well budded out,
  By the work of our Lord's hand.

3

Go down in your dairy and fetch me a cup,
  A cup of your sweet cream,*
And, if I should live to tarry in the town,
  I will call on you next year.

4

The hedges and the fields they are so green,
  As green as any leaf,
Our Heavenly Father waters them
  With His Heavenly dew so sweet.

5

When I am dead and in my grave,
  And covered with cold clay,
The nightingale will sit and sing,
  And pass the time away.

6

Take a Bible in your hand,
  And read a chapter through,
And, when the day of Judgment comes,
  The Lord will think on you.

7

I have a bag on my right arm,
  Draws up with a silken string,
Nothing does it want but a little silver
  To line it well within.

8

And now my song is almost done,
  I can no longer stay,
God bless you all both great and small,
  I wish you a joyful May.

[*Sung near Hinwick.*]

* ? cheer.

The Lost Lady found.

[DORIAN.] [LINCOLNSHIRE.]

Allegro. *ben marcato e con ballare.*

1. 'Twas down in a val-ley a fair maid did dwell, She lived with her un-cle, as all knew full well. 'Twas down in the val-ley, where vi-o-lets were gay, Three gyp-sies be-trayed her, and stole her a-way!

3. The trus-tee spake up, with a cour-age so bold, "I fear she's been lost for the sake of her gold; So we'll have life for life, sir," the trus-tee did say, "We shall send you to pris-on, and there you shall stay."

H.5873.

2. Long time she'd been miss_ing, and could not be found; Her un_cle he search_èd the coun_try a_round, Till he came to her trus_tee be_tween hope and fear, The trus_tee made an_swer "She has not been here!"

4. There was a young squi_re that lov_èd her so, Oft times to the school_house to_geth_er they did go; "I'm a_fraid she is mur_dered; so great is my fear, If I'd wings like a dove, I would fly to my dear!"

88

Omit from A to B if desired.

5. He travelled through England, through France and through Spain, Till he ventured his life on the watery main; And he came to a house where he lodged for a night, And in that same house was his own heart's delight.

7. "Your uncle's in England, in prison doth lie; And for your sweet sake is condemned for to die." "Carry me to old England, my dearest," she cried; "One thousand I'll give you and will be your bride."

H.5873.

6. When she saw him, she knew him, and flew to his arms, She told him her grief while he gazed on her charms. "How came you to Dublin, my dearest, I pray?" "Three gypsies betrayed me, and stole me away."

8. When she came to old England, her uncle to see, The cart it was under the high gallows tree. "Oh, pardon! oh, pardon! oh, pardon! I crave! Don't you see I'm alive, your dear life for to save?"

Omit from A to B if desired.

9. Then straight from the gallows they led him away, The bells they did ring, and the music did play; Ev'ry house in the valley with mirth did resound, As soon as they heard the lost lady was found.

simile

1

'Twas down in a valley a fair maid did dwell,
She lived with her uncle, as all knew full well;
'Twas down in the valley, where violets were gay,
Three gypsies betrayed her and stole her away.

2

Long time she'd been missing and could not be found,
Her uncle, he searchèd the country around,
Till he came to her trustee, between hope and fear,
The trustee made answer "She has not been here."

3

The trustee spake up with a courage so bold,
"I fear she's been lost for the sake of her gold;
So we'll have life for life, sir," the trustee did say,
"We shall send you to prison, and there you shall stay."

4

There was a young squire that lovèd her so,
Oft times to the schoolhouse together they did go;
"I'm afraid she is murdered; so great is my fear,
If I'd wings like a dove I would fly to my dear!"

5

He travelled through England, through France and through Spain,
Till he ventured his life on the watery main;
And he came to a house where he lodged for a night,
And in that same house was his own heart's delight.

6

When she saw him, she knew him, and flew to his arms,
She told him her grief while he gazed on her charms.
"How came you to Dublin, my dearest, I pray?"
"Three gypsies betrayed me, and stole me away."

7

"Your uncle's in England; in prison doth lie,
And for your sweet sake is condemned for to die."
"Carry me to old England, my dearest," she cried;
"One thousand I'll give you, and will be your bride."

8

When she came to old England, her uncle to see,
The cart it was under the high gallows tree.
"Oh, pardon! oh, pardon! oh, pardon! I crave!
Don't you see I'm alive, your dear life to save?"

9

Then straight from the gallows they led him away,
The bells they did ring, and the music did play;
Every house in the valley with mirth did resound,
As soon as they heard the lost lady was found.

[Sung by Mrs Hill, 1893.]

Died of Love
or
A brisk young Lad he courted me.

[DORIAN.] [NORTH LINCOLNSHIRE]

Andante espressivo.

sempre legato

A brisk young lad came court-ing me, He stole a-way my li-ber-ty; He stole my heart with a free good will,...... He has...... it

※ More often the C was made a minim and the D a crotchet, but the above, noted once, has been chosen as especially beautiful.

H.5873.

now, and he'll keep...... it still. There is a flow'r, I've heard them say, Would ease my heart............ both night and day; I......... would, to God, that flow'r I could find That would ease........... my heart, and my trou _ bling mind! Dig me my grave both wide and deep; Set a marble stone at my head and feet; And a turtle-white dove carve o-ver a-bove To let the world know that I died of love.

1

A brisk young lad came courting me,
He stole away my liberty;
He stole my heart with a free good will,
He has it now, and he'll keep it still.

2

There is a flower, I've heard them say,
Would ease my heart both night and day;
I would, to God, that flower I could find
That would ease my heart, and my troubling mind!

3

Dig me my grave both wide and deep;
Set a marble stone at my head and feet;
And a turtle-white dove carve over above,
To let the world know that I died of love.

[*Sung by M*^r *Joseph Taylor, of Saxby-All-Saints, 1906.*]

King Henry, my Son.

[ÆOLIAN.] [CUMBERLAND.]

Moderato.

1. "Oh, where have you been wan-d'ring, King Henry, my son? Where have you been wan-d'ring, my pretty one?" I've been to my sweetheart's, mother; make my bed soon, For I'm sick to the heart, and would fain lay me down!"

2. "And what did she give you, King Henry, my son? Oh, what did she give you, my pretty one?" "She fried me some †paddocks, mother; make my bed soon, For I'm sick to the heart, and would fain lay me down!"

† Old English for "toads."

più mosso e agitato
"And what will you leave your sweet_heart, King Hen - ry, my
sempre legato e dolce
pp una corda
son? Oh,..... what will you leave you sweet_heart, my..... pret - ty -
tre corde
one?" "My.... gar - ter, to hang her, mo_ther! make my bed
ff
ad libitum.
pp
ff colla voce
Ped. * Ped. *
soon, For I'm sick to.... the heart; I would fain lay me down."
cresc.
ppp rit.
colla voce
f

1

"Oh, where have you been wandering, King Henry, my son?
Where have you been wandering, my pretty one?"
"I've been to my sweetheart's, mother; make my bed soon,
For I'm sick to the heart, and would fain lay me down."

2

"And what did she give you, King Henry, my son?
Oh! what did she give you, my pretty one?"
"She fried me some *paddocks, mother; make my bed soon,
For I'm sick to the heart, and would fain lay me down."

3

"And what will you leave your sweetheart, King Henry, my son?
Oh! what will you leave your sweetheart, my pretty one?"
"My garter to hang her, mother! make my bed soon,
For I'm sick to the heart, I would fain lay me down."

[*Air, with a longer version of the ballad, sung by Miss Margaret Scott, some years before 1868.*]

*Old English for "toads"

See Appendix page 124.

Travel the Country round.

[SUSSEX.]

Allegro.

I am a jo_vial ran_ger, I fear_ no kind of danger; To sor_row I'm a stran_ger, And so let mirth a_bound......... I once had a fit of lov_ing, But, that con_tra_ry prov_ing, It set my mind a_rov_ing To tra_vel the coun_try round!...........

101

1.
I am a jovial ranger,
I fear no kind of danger,
To sorrow I'm a stranger,
   And so let mirth abound.
I once had a fit of loving,
But, that contrary proving,
It set my mind a-roving
   To travel the country round!

2.
When first of all I started,
From all my friends I parted,
All almost broken hearted,
   Alas! what grief I found!
Till London had fairly touched me,
No part of comfort reached me,
*The devil had surely bewitched me
   To travel the country round!

3.
When up to London I wandered
A deal of money I squandered,
I masters tried a hundred,
   No work was to be found.
And as I wandered up and down,
Some called me "a fool", some "country clown",
And bade me get out of their fine town
   To travel the country round!

4.
Now I grew quite dejected,
As well might be expected,
Myself I then directed
   To Reading, and was "bound".
As soon as I had arrived there,
Some work for me was contrived there,
And I for awhile was depriv'd there,
   From trav'lling the country round!

5.
Six months, or more, I tarried,
Till of Reading I grew wearied,
My roaming fancy fired
   To see some other town.
To Oxford then I hasted,
A week or more I wasted,
As long as my money lasted
   I travelled the country round.

6.
So now in Oxford my station;
And here, to my vexation,
A foolish new temptation
   To rest awhile I found.
A maid I met so pretty,
So good, so wise, so witty,
I thought it were surely a pity
   To travel the country round.

7.
Now I the case must alter,
For fear that I should falter,
And be led in a halter
   To church (a dismal sound!)
I made a resolution,
Which I put in execution,
It suited my constitution
   To travel the country round.

8.
So now †at home I'm seated,
My travels are all completed,
These words I have repeated,
   So awhile I'll sit me down;
Quite cured of all my moving,
As well as of all my loving,
I'll go no more a roving
   To travel the country round.

[*Sung by M*^r *H. Burstow, 1893.*]

* or "Old Harry."

† The singer substitutes the name of the nearest town for "at home."

H. 5873.

Oh, Yarmouth is a pretty Town.

[SUSSEX.]

Andante.

mf

legato *p*

Oh, Yar-mouth is a pret-ty town, And shines where it stands, And the more I think of it The more it runs in my mind; The

H.5873.

more I...... think of it It...... makes my heart.... to grieve. At the sign of..... the.... "An‿gel" Pret‿ty Nan‿cy...... did.... live.

più animato.

mf marcato.

The rout came on.... Sun‿day, On.... Mon‿day we march'd a‿way; The drums they did beat, And the music did play. Many hearts were rejoicing, But my heart was sad, To part from my true love What a full heart I had!

Will you go on.... board of ship? My.... love will.......... you try? I'll buy you as fine sea-fare As... mo-ney... will..... buy; And whilst I'm.... on...... sen-try I'll.... guard you from all.... foe! My love, will you go..... with me? But her an-swer was... "No!" Oh,

Yarmouth is a pretty town, And shines where it stands, And the more I think of it, The more it runs in my mind; The more I think of it, It makes my heart to grieve, At the sign of the "Angel" Pretty Nan I did leave.

1.
Oh, Yarmouth is a pretty town,
   And shines where it stands,
And the more I think of it
   The more it runs in my mind;
The more I think of it
   It makes my heart to grieve,
At the sign of the "Angel"
   Pretty Nancy did live.

2.
The rout came on Sunday,
   On Monday we march'd away:
The drums they did beat,
   And the music did play.
Many hearts were rejoicing,
   But my heart was sad,
To part from my true love
   What a full heart I had!

3.
Will you go on board of ship?
   My love, will you try?
I'll buy you as fine seafare
   As money will buy.
And whilst I'm on sentry
   I'll guard you from all foe!
My love, will you go with me?
   But her answer was "No!"

4.
Oh, Yarmouth is a pretty town,
   And shines where it stands,
And the more I think of it
   The more it runs in my mind;
The more I think of it
   It makes my heart to grieve,
At the sign of the "Angel"
   Pretty Nan I did leave.

[*Sung by Mr H. Burstow, 1893*]

Some rival has stolen my true love away.

[SURREY.]

Allegro moderato.

Some rival has stolen my true love away, So I in old England no longer can stay, I will swim the wide ocean all round {by/my} fair {Brest/breast} To find out my true love whom I love the best. When I have found out my true love and delight, I'll welcome her kindly by day or by night; For the bell shall be a-ringing, and the drums make a noise, To welcome my true love with ten thousand joys.

Here's a health to all lovers that are loyal and just! Here's confusion to the rival that lives in distrust! But it's I'll be as constant as a true turtle dove, For I never will at no time prove false to my love.

1.

Some rival has stolen my true love away,
So I in Old England no longer can stay;
I will swim the wide ocean all round {by / my} fair {Brest, / breast,}
To find out my true love whom I love best.

2.

When I have found out my true love and delight,
I'll welcome her kindly by day or by night;
For the bells shall be a-ringing, and the drums make a noise,
To welcome my true love with ten thousand joys.

3.

Here's a health to all lovers that are loyal and just!
Here's confusion to the rival that lives in distrust!
But it's I'll be as constant as a true turtle dove,
For I never will, at no time, prove false to my love.

[*Sung by Mr Lough, Dunsfold, 1898.*]

APPENDIX.

VAN DIEMEN'S LAND (p. 2).

This ballad is much like a broadside formerly printed by H. Such, Union St., Borough, with the same title. The broadside is if anything rather less grammatical, however. Such also printed a broadside called "The Gallant Poachers." These, and Fortey's broadside, "Young Henry, the Poacher," are all distinct ballads setting forth the woes of the poacher when caught. The English first colonised Van Diemen's Land (now Tasmania), in 1803. From 1804 to 1853 convicts were transported to the island. Possibly the words "hid in sand" may originally have been "hideous hand." For another melody see "Van Diemen's Land" in *The Complete Petrie Collection* (Boosey & Co.).

THE BOLD PEDLAR AND ROBIN HOOD (p. 4).

The words here given were, until quite lately, printed on broadsides by Such, and are much the same as those in Bell's *Songs of the Peasantry* (1857). Catnach, in the early part of the 19th century, printed a similar ballad. It is not to be found in Ritson's collection, or in the numerous Robin Hood Garlands. The story, however, is in its essentials the same as that of "Robin Hood and the Stranger" (*see* under "Robin Hood newly Revived" in Child's *English and Scottish Popular Ballads*). In the latter ballad "Gamble Gold" appears as "Gamwell," both names being a corruption of "Gamelyn," the hero of the manuscript *Tale of Gamelyn*, which Skeat believes to have been composed in 1340. There is also a ballad in the Sloane MS. (*circa* 1450), about "Robyn and Gandeleyn," which seems to refer to Robin Hood and Gamelyn.

THROUGH MOORFIELDS (p. 6).

Pitt, the ballad-printer, published very similar words in a penny book (*circa* 1830), "The Lover's Harmony." His version is evidently taken from a broadside of much earlier date; it has nine stanzas. The hero is a sailor.

Mad songs were the fashion in the 17th and 18th centuries. For further notes, and traditional examples, see *Journal of the Folk Song Society*, Vol. ii., p. 326 [Subject Index, "Madness"], and Vol. iii., p. 111; also "Bedlam City" and "The Loyal Lover" in *English County Songs*. "The Loyal Lover" is a curtailed version of a lengthy broadside called "Bedlam Walks." Giordani set "Bedlam Walks" to music which has absolutely nothing in common with the traditional airs above quoted.

The old Bethlem Hospital was removed from Bishopsgate Without to Moorfields, in 1675, and was again removed in 1814. The tune here given was noted by Mr. Buttifant, late organist of Horsham Parish Church, in 1893, and is faithfully accurate to the version then sung by Mr. Burstow, as heard by the editor. The variants printed show the alterations made by the same singer, and recorded by phonograph in 1907, after an interval of fourteen years.

BRISTOL TOWN (p. 10).

In the *Douce* Collection, Vol. iii. (Bodleian Library), there is a 17th century broadside, "The Bristol Bridegroom, or the Ship's Carpenter's Love to the Merchant's Daughter." This has 35 verses, the second of which is much the same as the first verse of the ballad here printed. (For a similar ballad see also *A choice Collection of New Songs*, Tewkesbury, *circa* 1790, Brit. Mus. 11,621, C. 1). The whole *plot* of this lengthy ballad is that of "The Valiant Lady, or the Brisk Young Lively Lad" in this collection (see p. 72), but the *Douce* ballad has stanzas in common with both songs, showing how strangely fluid old ballads have been for centuries. The tune here given with accompaniment, is as noted from Mr. Burstow's singing in 1893, by the editor on two occasions, and by Mr. J. A. Fuller Maitland on one occasion. In 1907, at the age of 82, Mr. Burstow sang the song into the phonograph, with very interesting variants which had established themselves during the interval of fourteen years. The words (printed in the *Journal of the Folk Song Society*, Vol. i., No. 4, from the singer's own writing), had also undergone slight changes, some of which have been used here as improvements. The whole song is of such interest that it is here given full length, from the phonograph-record taken by Dr. R. Vaughan Williams, which he has kindly allowed me to transcribe.

It will be observed that the cadence in verse 1 of the harmonised version, which was *most* persistently used in 1893, was not sung at all in 1907, unless perhaps at the end of the song, where the record is indistinct but suggests the possibility of its use. In 1893 the cadence used in verses 1 and 2 of the phonographed version was sung *occasionally*, and the cadence used *most* often in 1907 occurred so very seldom in 1893 as to seem an accidental "sport" at that time. Some of the variants in the latest version suggest that the old voice unconsciously, but artistically, had adapted the intervals to its powers. It is interesting to note that in the last verse the flat seventh was raised, and sung an almost pure C sharp, as if the tired singer found it less of an effort to sing a semitone than a whole tone at that point.

BRISTOL TOWN.

From Phonograph Record, 1907.

In Bristol Town as I have heard tell, A rich merchant there did dwell. He had a daughter beautiful and bright,........ On her he fixed his own heart's delight. Courtèd she was by many in the town, Courtèd she was by many a clever man; Courtèd she was by many a clever man,........... But none could this young lady's heart gain. Till a brisk young sailor he came from the seas, He did the lady well please. He was a brisk young man although a sailor poor,........... And the lady did the sailor adore. And when her father came to be told She was courtèd by this jolly sailor bold: "No! never, never, Oh! while I do live............ Not any portion unto you I'll give!" "As for your portion I do not care, I'll wed the man whom I love so dear. I'll wed the man that I...... do love so,............. If a-long with him to beg-ging I go!"

Her fa-ther kept a va-liant ser-vant man, Who wrote a let-ter out of......... hand. This

let-ter was the sail-or to in-vite............ To meet the la-dy in the val-ley by night.

Then her fa-ther kept a va-liant I-rish-man, And fif-ty pounds he gave him out of

hand, And a brace of poc-ket pis-tols like-wise....... He mounted, and a-way he did ride.

He mounted, and a-way he did ride, Till at length the jol-ly sail-or he es-pied, At

length the jol-ly sail-or he spied there........... A-wait-ing for his joy...... and his dear.

He said, "I am come to kill you in-deed! But a-way! back to some tav-ern with speed! Cheer

up your heart with bowls of good wine........... And soon I'll make you know my de-sign:

I'll go back to my mas-ter with speed, Say-ing, 'Mas-ter, I have killed that man in-

| *Record incomplete here.* |

-deed! I have bur-ied him all in his grave so low,......... Where streams and . . . .'"

In course of time this rich mer-chant died, Which filled the la-dy's heart full with pride. Now she's

| *faint and uncertain.* |

mar-ried to that man you know so brave,......... Who her fa-ther thought was dead and in his grave.

I MUST LIVE ALL ALONE (p. 16).

Verses 1, 2 and 3, here given, are essentially the same as the first three of the five stanzas sung. Verse 4 has been partly rewritten, whilst preserving the general idea of the original 5th. An early broadside, formerly in the possession of the Revd. S. Baring Gould, has very similar words, beginning, "One morning of late, as I walked in great state, I heard a maid making sad moan."

ROSETTA AND HER GAY PLOUGHBOY (p. 18).

The singer's version of words hardly varies from that on Such's broadside of the same name. Cf. the execution ballad-air "Eli Sykes," *Journal of the Folk Song Society*, Vol. i., p. 244. Catnach's ballad of "Bold William Taylor" is sometimes sung to a similar type of tune. But a remarkably interesting likeness exists between the Sussex air and Air vii. in the Ballad Opera of *Silvia* (1731). The latter is called "Bell Chimes" and the words begin "Neighbours all, behold with sorrow."

"*Bell Chimes.*"

THE AGES OF MAN (p. 20).

See *Douce* and *Pepys* Collections for black letter broadsides of 12 stanzas (ten lines in each), called "The Age and Life of Man." These are illustrated with Jacobean woodcuts. The ballad begins "As I was wandering all alone," and on the *Douce* copy is stated to be "by P. Fancy." It is directed to be sung to the tune "Jane Shore." Williamson, Cole, Wright, etc., published these. Thackeray in the reign of Charles II. also printed "The Life and Age of Man" on broadsides; and, until lately, Such printed "The Seven Ages of Man," very similar to this version and to that in Bell's *Songs of the Peasantry* (1857), but rather more corrupted. The fine tune, previously sung to the editor, was noted by Mr. Buttifant, late organist of Horsham Parish Church. In the Ballad Opera of *Silvia* (1731) there is a minor tune (Air xiv.) called "The State of Man," which, rhythmically, suggests that it was used for similar words to those here given.

THE DUKE OF MARLBOROUGH (p. 22).

Cf. "Marlborough" in Barrett's *English Folk Songs*. The singer's version of words followed the broadside (till lately still printed by Such), here given. Harkness of Preston printed similar words. The ballad is a great favourite amongst country people; the airs sung to it are usually very fine, and most often modal. For another air *see* "Lord Melbourne," *Journal of the Folk Song Society*, Vol. iii., No. 12.

THE WEALTHY FARMER'S SON (p. 26).

Cf. the tune with "The Honest Ploughman" in Barrett's *English Folk Songs*, and "The Besom Maker" in Heywood Sumner's *Besom Maker*. Such prints the words. The tune was also noted by Mr. Buttifant, late organist of Horsham Parish Church.

THE MERCHANT'S DAUGHTER, OR CONSTANT FARMER'S SON (p. 28).

The words are on ballad-sheets by Such and other printers. They should be compared with those of "Bruton Town" (*Folk Songs from Somerset*, Series i.). Both ballads have for their plot a story strangely like that in Boccaccio's *Decameron*, which, though versified in delightful and homely fashion by Hans Sachs, is chiefly familiar to English readers through Keats' poem "Isabella and the Pot of Basil."

"Bruton Town" has many more points of likeness to Boccaccio's story than has the foregoing ballad; but it is possible that both the Somerset and Sussex versions are based on the old tale, seeing that Boccaccio's "Story of Patient Grisilda" survives in doggerel form on a broadside of the 17th century (see *Roxburghe Coll.*), and that the classics provided much material for the early ballad-makers.

HENRY MARTIN (p. 30).

For full notes on this ballad, and an air, see "Henry Martyn" and "Sir Andrew Barton" in Child's *English and Scottish Ballads*. The words here given are probably from Catnach's broadside. For other versions see *Songs of the West*, Kidson's *Traditional Tunes*, and *Folk Songs from Somerset*. Child writes: "In the year 1476 a Portuguese squadron seized a richly loaded ship commanded by John Barton, in consequence of which letters of reprisal were granted to Andrew, Robert, and John Barton, sons of John, and these letters were renewed in 1506, 'as no opportunity had occurred of effectuating a retaliation'; that is to say, as the Scots, up to the later date, had not been supplied with the proper vessels. The King of Portugal remonstrated, ... but he had put himself in the wrong four times."
There is reason, however, to think that the Bartons abused the Royal favour, and converted "this retaliation into a kind of piracy against the Portuguese trade, at that time, by the discoveries and acquisitions in India, rendered the richest in the world." All three brothers were men of note in the naval history of Scotland. See Hall's Chronicle, 1548, and old Scottish Chronicles.

GEORGIE, OR BANSTEAD DOWNS (p. 32).

For exhaustive notes on the ballad "Georgie," see Child's *English and Scottish Popular Ballads*, and *Journal of the Folk Song Society*. There are Scotch and English versions, totally distinct, yet here and there having a verse in common. The Scottish "Geordie" does not figure as a thief, as does the English. The Sussex version here given is, in subject and two stanzas, like "A lamentable new ditty made upon the death of a worthy gentleman named George Stoole, dwelling sometime on Gate-side Moore, and sometime at New-Castle in Northumberland: with his penitent end. To a delicate Scottish Tune." (*Roxburghe Coll.* i. 186, 187, &c.). There is also "The Life and Death of George of Oxford. To a pleasant tune called Poor Georgy." (*Roxburghe Coll.* iv. 53, &c., printed between 1671 and 1692). Its first stanza, beginning "As I went over London Bridge," is much the same as the first verse of "Banstead Downs," and two or three other verses have points common to both ballads. "George of Oxford" is hung in "a silken string." George Stoole (see "Georgie" in Kidson's *Traditional Tunes*) was executed in 1610. See Christie's *Ballads*, Johnson's *Scots Musical Museum*, Hogg's *Jacobite Relics*, and *Folk Songs from Somerset* for other airs. Such, until lately, printed a broadside "The Life of Georgey." In the many versions Georgie is said to have sold the King's horses or deer to "Bohemia," "Bohenny," "Bevany," "Bennavie," and "Gory." Possibly "Germanie" may be nearer the original, which is usually meant to rhyme with the word "any" ("money" in the Sussex version).

BONEY'S LAMENTATION (p. 34).

In this ballad, the singer, whilst preserving the correct sequence of events, corrupted the names of persons and places very puzzlingly. These have now been carefully restored in the light of history (cf. original words in *Journal of the Folk Song Society*, No. 4.) The misplacement of several sentences has been adjustable by help of the triple rhymes. The Lamentation ends with Napoleon's abdication, and, as the battle of Waterloo is not mentioned, we may infer that the ballad was composed in the year 1814.

The air of "Boney's Lamentation" is a variant of the famous old tune "the Princess Royal," popular in England, and in print in English books, already about the year 1727. Shield "adapted" and "arranged" the tune (which is erroneously attributed to him by most editors), for the sea song "The Arethusa" in Prince Hoare's opera called "The Lock and Key," produced 1796. In O'Farrell's *Pocket Companion* (*circa* 1810), the air is described as "by Carolan" (the Irish harpist, 1670-1738.) Bunting repeats this statement, for which there seems no foundation, in his *Ancient Irish Music* (1840.) Full and very interesting notes, and examples of the tune in its early printed forms, are given by Mr. Frank Kidson under the title "The Arethusa" in *English Songs of the Georgian Period*, edited by A. Moffat. The traditional tune here given has modal points which are absent in the airs as usually printed. Henry Burstow learned the song first when a child of six, from his father.

BELFAST MOUNTAINS (p. 36).

The words follow very closely those on a ballad-sheet (*circa* 1800), printed by W. Shelmerdine, Manchester. Catnach also printed a version. There is a popular Irish superstition that Cave Hill near Belfast contains diamonds which shine sometimes at night, and this throws light upon similar allusions to diamonds, found so frequently in Irish broadsides of a particular type. Cf. "Faithful Emma" in *English County Songs*, and "Come all you little Streamers," *Journal of the Folk Song Society*, Vol, i., p. 122, also "The Belfast Mountains," *Complete Petrie Collection* (Boosey) No. 558.

THE YOUNG SERVANT MAN (p. 38).

In Bunting's *Ancient Music of Ireland* (1840), there is a tune communicated by Petrie, called "A Sailor wooed a Farmer's Daughter," which Sir C. V. Stanford has included (with modern words), in *Songs of Old Ireland*. It has some likeness to the air of "The Young Servant Man," though Sir C. V. Stanford considers the latter to be distinctly English in character. Compare "You Maidens Pretty" in *Songs of the West*. Catnach, and other printers, published a very similar ballad, sometimes under the title of "The Cruel Father and Affectionate Lover." For interesting variants see *Journal of the Folk Song Society*, Nos. 4, 7, and 10. The time is usually irregular, and not often so well defined as in the version here given.

DEATH AND THE LADY (p. 40).

This is a fine version of a very early moral ballad. The subject of "The Dance of Death," and dialogues between Death and his victims were popular throughout civilised Europe in the 14th and 15th centuries. Similar dialogues were still in great favour amongst ballad-singers of the 18th century. Judging from the present habit of country singers, who often act dialogue-songs, one may infer that the ballad of "Death and the Lady" was sometimes acted by two singers. Certainly the very similar dialogue between "Death and the Miser" formed part of an open air stage-play acted by Shropshire country-folk within memory of people still living (see *Shropshire Folk Lore* by C. Burne). Henry Carey, in his musical burlesque *A New Year's Ode* (1737), uses for a *recitative a tune which is distinctly a variant of the Sussex air here given, and he heads it "The Melody stolen from an old ballad called Death and the Lady." Carey's tune is reproduced in *Journal of the Folk Song Society*, Vol. ii., p. 138. Another distinct variant is printed both in *The Cobler's Opera* (1729), and another ballad-opera, *The Fashionable Lady* (1730), to quite new words, though a line or two in the latter opera's libretto slightly parody one verse of "Death and the Lady." Much of interest concerning the ballad may be read in Chappell's *Popular Music*, where yet another variant of the same tune is given. It is greatly to be regretted, however, that Chappell does not give (nor can his editor, Mr. Wooldridge, supply) the source of his tune, which is not at all identical with either Carey's version or that in the above-named ballad-operas, though all three sources are referred to by him. Chappell may have taken it from some other opera of the same date. The editor has, so far, been unable to find the tune associated in print with its own dialogue of "Death and the Lady." In the *Pepys*, *Douce* and *Roxburghe* Collections there are broadsides of the 17th century, which differ considerably from each other, are very irregular in construction, but are much on the lines of the traditional version here printed. See "The Great Messenger of Mortality, or a Dialogue betwixt Death and a Lady" (*Roxburghe* Coll.) and "The Messenger of Mortality" in Bell's *Ballads and Songs of the Peasantry* (1859), which is remarkably like both the Sussex version and one quoted by Chappell in his *Ancient English Ballads* (1840), from a broadside printed in Seven Dials. In the *Bagford* Ballads is a dialogue "betwixt an Exciseman and Death" (1659). Mr. Burstow's version is a wonderful proof of a country singer's memory. Lately (1908), at the age of 83, he sang it all through without a slip, and with every word precisely as here given. Some of his lines seem an improvement on the printed broadside versions. He however despises the tune, as being "almost all on one note." In *Songs of the West* and *Folk Songs from Somerset* there is an entirely different ballad called "Death and the Lady," with altogether different tunes.

---

* The air here printed should also be sung with considerable freedom as regards the relative value of the notes.

THE THREE BUTCHERS, OR GIBSON, WILSON, AND JOHNSON (p. 42).

This is a version of an old ballad found in various forms on black-letter and white-letter broadsides of the 17th century (*Roxburghe, Pepys*, and *Douce Collections*, etc.). One copy (*Rox. Coll.* iii., 30, iv., 80), is called "The Three Worthy Butchers of the North. To a pleasant new Tune." This has ten stanzas of ten lines each; and choruses, used only in first and last verse, which run "*With a hey down down, with a down derry dee, God bless all true men out of Thieves' company*," and "*God bless all true men that travel by Land and Sea, And keep all true men out of Thieves' company!*" Contrary to the usual custom in broadsides, the author's name, Paul Burges, is appended. In this version the butchers' names are "Kitson, Wilson, and Johnson," and we learn that they were "riding thorow Blankly-lane" when the treacherous woman-thief screamed. The prudent Kitson, having often ridden that way and heard the same scream before, suspects a company of robbers; but the worthy Johnson declares that he cannot let a woman perish, and flies to her rescue. He finds her bound with cords, she says by highwaymen who have just robbed her. He cuts the cords, and is so moved with pity that he cries, "I have neither wife nor children......And thou shalt be the Lady of all, till death take life away." In the final tragedy the woman, having "knock'd him down behind," takes a club and dashes out the brains of Kitson and Wilson "where they lay bound in woe," exclaiming "They were cowards—and as cowards they shall die!" A "silly shepherd, hid in the hedge for fear," at once "sent forth hue and cry, To a gentleman and his man as they came riding by," but the thieves "got ship at Yarmouth" and escaped.

A second version (*Roxburghe Coll.* iii., 496), has the title "A New Ballad of the Three Merry Butchers, etc., etc., etc. To an excellent New Tune." It has eleven verses of four lines each, and a chorus "With a high ding, ding, with a ho ding ding, with a high ding, ding dee, And God bless all good people from evil company." The names are "Wilson, Gibson, and Johnson." This is very much like the Sussex traditional version. The words "squeaking" and "screeking" in the old broadsides are preserved as "screekful" in the Sussex ballad.

Such and Catnach issued a modern ballad-sheet "Ips, Gips, and Johnson, or the Three Butchers." This has eight verses of four lines, and no chorus. It is less like the second Roxburghe ballad than is the Sussex version, and it gives Northumberland as the scene of action. Probably the story is genuine history. Certainly the butchers' names, preserved in all variants, are amongst the commonest in Northumberland to this day. On the other hand, "Blankly-lane" and "the Land's-end" mentioned in the first Roxburghe ballad are thought, by the editor of the *Ballad Society's* reprint, to be "Blakeney" near a "Land's-end" promontory, at the mouth of the River Glaven in Norfolk. Thence the thieves would naturally escape by way of Yarmouth. The song (to a tune unfortunately not noted) was invariably sung at parish functions by an old inhabitant at Wretham, Norfolk, within the last fifteen years or so, to the editor's own knowledge; and versions, to several distinct tunes, have been recovered by recent collectors in Hampshire and Dorsetshire. The editor has not, so far, met with the Sussex tune elsewhere. It has some likeness to the air "Cupid's Garden."

THE UNQUIET GRAVE, OR COLD BLOWS THE WIND (pp. 50, 52, 54).

Mrs. Jeffreys' great age and ill-health made it impossible to note more than the tune and the two beautiful concluding verses here printed. The other verses were so much the same as in the Shropshire version (see *English County Songs*), that the latter has been re-printed here, up to the point where Mrs. Jeffreys' materially differed. Other tunes, versions of words, and references are in *Journal of the Folk Song Society*, Nos. 3, 4 and 6; *Folk Songs from Somerset;* and *Songs of the West.* In dealing with this, one of our most popular and most poetical traditional ballads, Child shows how ancient and universal is the idea that immoderate grief prevents the dead from resting. His great work on ballads should certainly be consulted on the subject. Mr. H. E. D. Hammond has noted in Dorsetshire the following interesting words, which come after "your time it won't be long":—

> "Let my time be long, or short, sweetheart,
>   Ay! then, to-day or to-morrow,
> I'll leave this world and all behind,
>   Nor leave it not in sorrow!"

> "Oh! don't you see the fire, sweetheart,
>   The fire that burns so blue?
> Whilst my poor soul's tormented here?
>   Whilst I remain with you?
>
> O down in yonder green, sweetheart,
>   Where you and I have walked," etc., etc.

Mrs. Rugman (see "Unquiet Grave" No. 2), sang as follows:—

> "Your lips they are as cold as clay,
>   Your breath it do smell strong."

This makes sense if put into the mouth of the girl, but spoils the flow of the verse, and is probably a corruption, as no other versions at present known seem to have it so.

OH, THE TREES ARE GETTING HIGH (p. 56).

This ballad is said to be founded on fact, and to date from the time when betrothals and marriages of mere children, "for convenience," were not uncommon. The "bonny boy" has been sometimes identified with young Urquhart of Craigston, who was married by the Laird of Innes to his daughter Elizabeth Innes, and died in 1634 (see "Lady Mary Anne" in Johnson's *Scots Musical Museum*, Vol. iv.), and a Scotch version has the title "Craigston's Growing." For other references and versions, tunes and words, see *Journal of the Folk Song Society*, Vol. i., p. 214, and Vol. ii., pp. 44, 95, and 206; *Songs of the West;* Christie's *Traditional Ballad Airs;* and *Folk Songs from Somerset*. A good version of words is on a broadside printed by Such and called "My Bonny Lad is young, but he's growing." The version here given was sung first to the editor by Mr. Ede whilst he was trimming hedges, and the fierce snap of his shears at the words "So there was an end of his growing" came with startling dramatic effect. A few words of Mr. Ede's version have been transposed or slightly altered where rhyme or metre absolutely necessitated it, and one stanza has been omitted. The original, however, is in *Journal of the Folk Song Society*, Vol. i., p. 214.

OUR SHIP SHE LIES IN HARBOUR (p. 58).

An equally doggerel version of the words is on a broadside printed by Such. After the fifth verse he prints the following:—

> When nine long years were over,
> And ten long tedious days,
> She saw the ship come sailing in
> With her true love from the seas.

The tune is sometimes used in Sussex to the words of the Sussex Mummers' Carol (see p. 80 of this collection). In two cases the singers sang F natural consistently.

THE IRISH GIRL (p. 60).

Almost identical words are on a broadside issued by Such, called "The New Irish Girl," the term "new" affixed to titles of the kind usually meaning that there has been an older ballad with a similar title. Disley, of St. Giles, printed another called "The Irish Girl." The Surrey singer's words have here been given. His is the only printed or traditional version known to the editor in which sense seems to be made of verse 3, by describing the suffering and broken-hearted "love" as a woman. The ballad, to a variety of very fine airs, is a great favourite with country singers. For major tunes, and variants of the words, see *Journal of the Folk Song Society*, Vol. i., p. 25, and the *Complete Petrie Collection* (Boosey), No. 535. An entirely different air from all these, and in the major, was printed by Skillern in the eighteenth century. Skillern, whose publications show that he had a taste for traditional song, calls this "The Irish Girl, a favorite Song." The first four lines of his first verse are much like the first four of the Surrey version. Skillern gives three stanzas of six lines each. Beyond this there is no close likeness, except that Skillern has the line "O love it is," etc.

His words have several lines in common with Petrie's version (*see* Old English Ballads formerly in Dr. Burney's library, B. Museum. G 306, Vol. i.). Yet another version of the same ballad, with six verses, is in a chap-book printed at Tewkesbury, about 1790, called "The Irish Girl" [B. Museum, 11,621, c.i.]. No two copies are alike, which demonstrates the extraordinary fluidity of popular ballads, and adds mystery to their original authorship.

THE LITTLE LOWLAND MAID (p. 66).

A broadside version, called "The Cruel Lowland Maid" and signed *G. Brown*, was printed by Ryle, successor to Catnach. The singer's words "courtmaid," "valliant," and "manastree" being obviously "comrade," "villain," and "monster," have been altered in the version here given.

THE POOR MURDERED WOMAN (p. 70).

This fine Dorian tune was noted in 1897 by the Rev. Charles J. Shebbeare at Milford, Surrey, from the singing of a young labourer, with whom it was a favourite song. Mr. Foster wrote out the doggerel words, and had heard that they described a real event. Through the kindness of the Vicar of Leatherhead, the Rev. E. J. Nash (who questioned Mr. Lisney, a parishioner of 87, in Feb. 1908), the ballad has proved to be an accurate account of the finding and burial (Jan. 15th, 1834,) of "a woman—name unknown—found in the common field," as the parish Registers give it. Mr. Lisney, who remembered the events perfectly, said that the author of the ballad was Mr. Fairs, a brickmaker of Leatherhead Common. The Milford labourer's version of names, "Yankee" for "Hankey," and "John Sinn," for "John Simms" of the Royal Oak Inn, are in *Journal of the Folk Song Society*, Vol. i, p. 186. His obscure line in verse 5 has here been altered to something probably more like the original, for "the poor woman's head had been broken with a stick." The Milford singer gave it: "Some old or some violence came into their heads." This song is only one of many proofs that "ballets" are made by local, untaught bards, and that they are transmitted, and survive, long after the events which they record have ceased to be a reality to the singer.

THE VALIANT LADY, OR THE BRISK YOUNG LIVELY LAD (p. 72).

This is a variant of a black-letter ballad "The Valiant Virgin, or Philip and Mary," etc., etc. "To the Tune of *When the Stormy Winds do blow*," [21 stanzas, *Roxburge Coll.*, ii, 546]. In this longer ballad we learn that the lady is a rich gentleman's daughter, well versed in surgery and medicine, and her lover a poor farmer's son, both of Worcestershire. Also that, her father dying whilst Philip and Mary are still at sea, they return to her estate "to marry, to the admiration of all those that were at the wedding," as the title says. Mr. Baker forgot two lines of verse 6, and these have been restored from the old broadside. Verse 4 has also been inserted from the black-letter copy, to explain the story. The older ballad shows signs of having itself been orally transmitted. The tune of "When the stormy winds do blow" was a very favourite ballad-air in the 17th century, and the title was used as a burden to many songs. Chappell, in *Popular Music*, gives a tune to "You Gentlemen of England," from a black-letter broadside, every verse of which ends "When the stormy winds do blow." The last bars of this tune are much like the last eight bars of the Surrey air here given; but, for the rest, Chappell's tune has little or no likeness, and is astonishingly weak and monotonous. In *English County Songs* there is a Gloucestershire "Shepherd's Song," with the burden "When the stormy winds do blow." This, when converted from six-eight into common time, shows a strong likeness to the Surrey tune; and, like it, is far more vigorous than Chappell's air. Chappell states that "No early copy of the tune is known." Possibly the Surrey and Gloucestershire traditional versions are more like the original favourite air than is the meaningless tune in *Popular Music*. In any case it is striking to find country labourers at the close of the 19th century singing a variant of a 17th century broadside to a version of its appointed air. As there is a strong likeness between the last eight bars of the song and the chorus of John Davy's famous "Bay of Biscay," it is well to repeat here the history of the latter: The great singer Incledon (1763–1826), whilst still in the Royal Navy, heard some drunken negro sailors shouting a chorus which took his fancy. This he repeated to Davy, who utilised it for his song to which Cherry wrote words. May the negroes not have been singing, "When the stormy winds do blow?"

KING PHARAOH, GYPSY CHRISTMAS CAROL (p. 74).

Child's *English and Scottish Ballads* should without fail be consulted for notes on the carols "St. Stephen and Herod" and the "Carnal and the Crane." The first-named is preserved in the British Museum, in a MS. judged to be of the time of Henry VI. It narrates that St. Stephen, dish-bearer to King Herod, sees the Star of Bethlehem, and tells the king that Christ is born. Herod scoffingly says that this is as likely as that the capon in the dish should crow. The capon thereupon rises, and crows "Christus natus est!" This legend is extremely ancient, and widely spread over Europe. Its source seems to be an interpolation in two late Greek MSS. of the so-called *Gospel of Nicodemus*. "The Carnal and the Crane" (see Sandys' *Christmas Carols* and Husk's *Songs of the Nativity*), appeared on broadsides of the middle of the eighteenth century. The well-informed crane instructs his catechumen, the carnal (*i.e.*, crow), in matters pertaining to the early days of Jesus; and tells how the wise men tried to convince Herod of the birth of Christ by the miracle of the roasted cock, which rose freshly feathered, and crowed in the dish. It also relates the legend of the Instantaneous Harvest, which occurs in Apocryphal Gospels (see B. Harris Cowper's *Apocryphal Gospels*). The carol consists of thirty stanzas, some of which have lines in common with the Surrey carol here given. It, likewise, is exceedingly corrupted and incoherent, and must have been transmitted orally from some very remote source. The singers of the Surrey version are very well known Gypsy tramps in the neighbourhood of Horsham and Dorking. "King Pharim" is of course a corruption of "King Pharaoh," and that name is properly given in a very interesting traditional version of "The Carnal and the Crane" lately noted in Herefordshire. It is quite natural that gypsies should substitute "Pharaoh" for "Herod," for, on the first appearance of gypsies in Europe (in the fifteenth century), the Church spread the legend that they came from Egypt with a curse upon them because they had refused to receive the Virgin and Child. The gypsies in time came to believe themselves Egyptians, and, according to Simson (1865), recognise Pharaoh as their former king. There is, however, an interesting allusion to Pharaoh in the Arabic *Gospel of the Infancy*, Chap. xxv.: "Thence they (Joseph, Mary and Jesus), went down to Memphis, and having seen Pharaoh they staid three years in Egypt; and the Lord Jesus wrought very many miracles in Egypt." The editor of the Gospel adds, "Memphis may have been visited, but who was Pharaoh? Egypt was then under Roman rule." The sixth verse of the "King Pharim" carol is a paraphrase of a passage in the Gospel of Pseudo-Matthew, Chap. xx.

THE MOON SHINES BRIGHT (p. 76).

Versions of this popular traditional carol, tunes and words widely differing, are in nearly every carol-book or collection of country songs, from Sandys' *Christmas Carols* (1833) onwards; amongst others, in C. Burne's *Shropshire Folk-Lore, English County Songs, Sussex Songs, Songs of the West*, Rimbault's *Carols*, Bramley and Stainer's *Carols*, and *Journal of the Folk Song Society*, Nos. 4 and 7. It is sung, with appropriate adaptations, either at Christmas time or on May Day. Hone states, in 1823, that it was one of the carols still annually printed on ballad-sheets. The sombre variant of words here given seems to be especially liked by gypsies (see the singularly interesting versions in *Shropshire Folk-Lore*, and *Notes and Queries*, 8th series, ii., Dec. 24, 1892). Compare the carols following in this collection.

THE HAMPSHIRE MUMMERS' CAROL (p. 78).

This was noted by Mr. Godfrey Arkwright. An error in the cadence, which was printed in the *Journal of the Folk Song Society*, Vol. i., No. 4, is here corrected.

SUSSEX MUMMERS' CAROL (p. 80).

This very beautiful carol was sung several years in succession by Christmas Mummers, also called in Sussex "Tipteers" or "Tipteerers," a name still unexplained in our dialect dictionaries. It was noted in 1880 and 1881, after which the Mummers ceased to act in the neighbourhood of Horsham. They clustered together, wooden swords in hand, at the close of their play "St. George and the Turk," and sang, wholly unconscious of the contrast between the solemnity of the carol and the grotesqueness of their appearance, for they wore dresses of coloured calico, and old "chimney-pot" hats, heavily trimmed with shreds of ribbon, gaudy paper fringes and odd ornaments.

Two actors in 1881 provided a few verses in very corrupted form. These were patched together by the present editor for the sake of including the carol in *Sussex Songs*. Fortunately, an appeal in the *West Sussex Gazette* in 1904 was answered by five village correspondents, who sent versions varying interestingly in detail, but agreeing in the main. From the seven copies this version was selected, as needing only very trifling emendations, which have been made in every case with the help of the other versions. In only one copy is the word "rood" rightly preserved to rhyme with "blood"; in other cases the modern word "cross" has been substituted. Three versions have a verse in which the angel addresses the Virgin. In one copy the master of the house is described as having "a gold chain round his waist." Similar words to a different tune have lately been noted from Hampshire Mummers. It is worth noting that the surname of the two actors in Sussex who first supplied fragments of the carol words was "Hampshire." The carol is sometimes sung in Sussex to the tune "Our ship she lies in harbour" (see p. 58 of this collection. For variants and further notes see *Journal of the Folk Song Society*, Vol. ii., No. 7, p. 128).

Singers who wish for a fuller accompaniment with fewer verses may have the beautiful arrangement by C. A. Lidgey, called "The Mummers' Carol" (Boosey & Co.).

BEDFORDSHIRE MAY DAY CAROL (p. 84).

This carol, contributed by Sir Ernest Clarke, is sung at Hinwick. It should be compared with "The Moon shines bright" and "The Hampshire Mummers' Carol." The words of course allude to the undoubtedly pagan May Day customs against which the Puritan Stubbes declaims in his *Anatomie of Abuses*, (1583). On the first day of May young men and women were wont to rise a little before midnight and to walk to some neighbouring wood, making music with horns and other instruments. There they would break boughs of hawthorn and other trees, weave garlands, and wander till sunrise, washing their faces in the May dew so magical in its properties. The boughs were then planted before the house-doors, and nosegays left at the thresholds; carols being sung, and gifts asked for in song. Countess Martinengo-Cesaresco, in her excellent *Essays in the Study of Folk Songs*, quotes the words of a March Day song sung by Greek children of Rhodes more than two thousand years ago. This, of which a version is sung still by Greek country folk, is strikingly like our May Day and Wassail Songs. It is supposed that the Puritans supplied the gloomy reminders of death in these Christmas and May Carols.

THE LOST LADY FOUND (p. 86).

Mrs. Hill, an old family nurse, and a native of Stamford, learned her delightful song when a child, from an old cook who danced as she sang it, beating time on the stone kitchen-floor with her iron pattens. The cook was thus unconsciously carrying out the original intention of the "ballad" which is the English equivalent of the Italian "balletta" (from *ballare*, "to dance") signifying a song to dance-measure, accompanied by dancing. The old English form of the word is "ballet," and country-singers invariably use this still. Mrs. Hill followed the ballad-sheet version printed by Such, which is here given. A different version of the ballad, to a good major tune, was noted by the Rev. John Broadwood before 1840 (*see Sussex Songs*). Other versions and tunes are in Barrett's *English Folk Songs*, and *Journal of the Folk Song Society*, Vol. ii, No. 7. Brock, of Bristol, printed a similar ballad in broadside form. The tune should be compared with that of "The Lament of the Duchess of Gloucester" (words modern), in Gill's *Manx National Songs* (Boosey & Co.), and with certain Dorian versions of "Green Bushes."

DIED OF LOVE (p. 92).

The singer remembered only two verses of words. Of these the first verse, though beautiful, is too painfully tragic for general use. It has therefore been omitted here, and two stanzas from a variant of a similar ballad, noted by Mr. H. E. D. Hammond in Dorsetshire, have by his kindness been used for verses 1 and 2. The words of this song belong to a type of ballad which is extraordinarily popular amongst country singers both in England and Scotland. The subject (of a forsaken and broken-hearted girl, who directs how her grave shall be made), is the same in all versions, which however vary astonishingly in detail, whilst having certain lines or stanzas always in common. For copious references, and various tunes, *see* Kidson's *Traditional Tunes*, "My True love once he courted me"; and *Journal of the Folk Song Society* under the titles of "Died for Love," "A Bold Young Farmer" (or "Sailor"), "In Jessie's City," "There is an Alehouse (or Tavern) in Yonder Town," etc. Usually the tunes sung to these ballads are especially beautiful, and most often modal. A much shortened version of the old words, set to a frankly modern and jingly air and chorus, is in the *Scottish Student's Song Book*, as "There is a Tavern in the Town." It is there described as "adapted from a Cornish folk song." This version has found its way into cheap sheet music form, Paxton printing it. Another edition, with more modernised words and slightly altered chorus, is published by Blockley, with "The Best of Friends must part" as its first title. In its jaunty modern form it is a great favourite amongst our soldiers.

The fine Dorian tune here given has striking points of likeness to the ancient "Song of Agincourt," thought to be a folk-tune (*see* Chappell's *Popular Music*). It was also noted by Mr. Percy Grainger, from the same singer *(see Journal of the Folk Song Society*, Vol. iii No. 12).

KING HENRY, MY SON (p. 96).

This ballad, in different forms, has been popular throughout Europe from early times, the poisoner usually being sweetheart or stepmother, and offering the most untempting food to the guest, such as a four-footed, blue-and-green, striped or speckled fish, speckled toads, eels, adders, snakes, and the like. In England and Scotland the ballad is best known as "Lord Randal, Rendel, or Ronald," "Lord Donald," "King Henry," and "the Croodlin' Doo'" (*i.e.*, "Cooing Dove"). Child's large edition of ballads should be consulted if possible, and also the *Journal of the Folk Song Society*, Vol. ii., No. 6, and Vol. iii., No. 10. In the latter journal Miss Gilchrist, by the help of an old peerage *The Catalogue of Honour* (1610), connects "Lord Randal" of the English ballad most interestingly with Randal iii., sixth Earl of Chester, who died in 1232. A summary of details, too lengthy to give here, is that "The fact, or story, that Randal's nephew and successor to the title was poisoned by his own wife may later have become attached to Randal himself." In Chappell's *Popular Music*, p. 10, there is an account of the services rendered by English minstrels to Randal when besieged in 1212. He is almost certainly the same popular hero as the person referred to by Langland (1362), whose Friar is more familiar with the "rimes of Robinhode and of Randal, erle of Chester," than with his Paternoster. In 1886 an Italian traditional version was still being sung in the district of Como. In this the lady poisons her lover, who bequeaths a tree to hang her. A similar ballad was known in Verona 250 years before that, and is referred to in literature of that time (see *Essays on the Study of Folk Songs*, by E. Martinengo-Cesaresco). Space only allows brief reference to the chief sources for studying this ballad. Smaller works, also containing versions, are Scott's *Minstrelsy of the Scottish Border*, *Folk Songs from Somerset*, *A Garland of Country Song*, and Johnson's *Scots Musical Museum*.

Miss M. B. Lattimer, living in Carlisle, noted this fine air, which she learned in childhood, some time before 1868, from Margaret Scott (now Mrs. Thorburn), a young servant in her home. The singer came from Wigton, in Cumberland, and had learnt the ballad from her father, who died when she was nine years old. Miss Lattimer recollected only a part of the words, and completed the ballad from another version, giving the three verses used in the harmonised arrangement. Recently, however, Miss Lattimer has come into communication with the singer, and received from her the following interesting set of words:—

KING HENRY, MY SON.

"Where have you been wandering, King Henry, my son?
Where have you been wandering, my pretty one?"
"I've been away hunting, mother, make my bed soon,
For I'm sick to the heart, and fain would lie down."

"What had you to your dinner, King Henry, my son?
What had you to your dinner, my pretty one?"
"A dish of small fishes, mother, make my bed soon,
For I'm weary, weary wandering, and fain would lie down."

"What colour was the fishes, King Henry, my son?
What colour was the fishes, my pretty one?"
"They were black bellies and speckled bellies, mother, make my bed soon,
"For I'm sick to the heart, and fain would lie down."

"I'm afraid you are poisoned, King Henry, my son,
   I'm afraid you are poisoned, my pretty one!"
"Yes, mother, I'm poisoned, make my bed soon,
   For I'm sick to the heart, and fain would lie down."

"What will you leave your mother, King Henry, my son?
   What will you leave your mother, my pretty one?"
"I will leave her my all—and make my bed soon,
   For I'm weary, weary wandering, and fain would lie down."

"What will you leave your brother, King Henry, my son?
   What will you leave your brother, my pretty one?"
"There's the best pair of horses, mother, make my bed soon,
   For I'm sick to the heart, and fain would lie down."

"What will you leave your sweetheart, King Henry, my son?
   What will you leave your sweetheart, my pretty one?"
"I will leave her my braces to hang her upon a tree;
   For the poisoning of my greyhounds, and the poisoning of me!"

O YARMOUTH IS A PRETTY TOWN (p. 102).

Verses 2 and 3 of the original (for which see *Journal of the Folk Song Society*, Vol. iii., No. 10) are here omitted, and verse 1 is repeated. The first line of the song, with different names for the town, is a favourite one on old broadsides. The ballad belongs to a class which shows affinity with "The Streams of Sweet Nancy," "The Boys of Kilkenny" (on which Moore founded his modern song), and "The Meeting of the Waters," pieces of which appear upon a number of old broadsides curiously and variously patched together. For very full notes on these *see* the above-mentioned Journal. The accompanist may bring out the quotations from "The British Grenadiers," "Rule Britannia," and "The Girl I left behind me" judiciously.

SOME RIVAL HAS STOLEN MY TRUE LOVE AWAY (p. 108).

In the *Roxburghe* Collection (*Ballad Society*. Vol. vi., pp. 67 and 69), there is a broadside, circa 1656, "Love's Fierce Desire, etc.: A true and brief Description of two resolved Lovers, etc." "To an excellent new Tune (its own) or, Fair Angel of England." This begins "Now the Tyrant hath stolen my dearest away." The suitor addresses the lady in seven stanzas, and she replies in eight verses, the second, third, and sixth of which have much similarity to the words of "Some Rival, etc." But the whole ballad is distinct, and artificial in character, and would seem to be based upon some older song. "I'll Swim through the Ocean upon my bare breast" is in the broadside, and appears to be correct. The Sussex singer's "my fair breast" suggested a possible corruption from "by fair Brest." In Playford's *Musical Companion* (1667) there is a different four-verse song, "Though the Tyrant hath ravished my dearest away." It has only the first line in common with the above ballads, but its tune (set for four voices), though a very poor one, has a distinct likeness to the Sussex traditional air. Other Sussex versions begin, "A merry King (of Old England) has stolen" and "The Americans have stolen." The ballad beginning "Fair Angel of England" (*see* beginning of this note) refers to the wooing of a "fair maid of London" by King Edward IV., who appears as an imperious and dangerously determined lover. Possibly he is the "Tyrant," "Merry King," and "Rival" referred to. A number of 17th century ballads are directed to be sung to the tune, "The Tyrant hath stolen." For further versions and notes see *Journal of the Folk Song Society*, Vol. i., No. 4, pp. 205, 208, and Vol. iii., No. 12.